The Battle
East of Elsenborn

In memory of my good friends.
The late Richard H. Byers and Rex W. Whitehead

The Battle
East of Elsenborn

and the Twin villages

WILLIAM C. C. CAVANAGH

Pen & Sword
MILITARY

Originally published in 1986 under the title
'Krinkelt – Rocherath, The Battle for the Twin Villages.'
by The Christopher Publishing House of Norwell Massachusetts.

Copyright © William C.C. Cavanagh, 2004

ISBN 1 84415 126 3

The right of William C.C. Cavanagh to be identified as Author
of this work has been asserted by him in accordance
with the Copyright, Designs and Patents Act 1988.

A CIP catalogue record for this book is
available from the British Library

Typeset in 10pt Plantin by Pen & Sword Books Limited

Printed and bound in England by
CPI UK

Pen & Sword Books Ltd incorporates the imprints of
Pen & Sword Aviation, Pen & Sword Maritime, Pen & Sword Military,
Wharncliffe Local History, Pen & Sword Select,
Pen & Sword Military Classics and Leo Cooper.

For a complete list of Pen & Sword titles please contact
PEN & SWORD BOOKS LIMITED
47 Church Street, Barnsley, South Yorkshire, S70 2AS, England
E-mail: enquiries@pen-and-sword.co.uk • website: www.pen-and-sword.co.uk

Contents

Foreword (1984)

By General, USA Retired Frank T. Mildren †
Former Commander
1st Battalion, 38th Infantry Regiment
2nd Infantry Division

In the forty years since Allied Expeditionary Forces assaulted Hitler's 'Fortress Europe', many books, histories and articles have been written concerning the Second World War campaigns. Most have covered the war in general, or have concentrated on large operations such as the Normandy landings or the 'Battle of the Bulge'. The author of this book has spent years of research on what was essentially a five-day critical battle for the north shoulder of the Bulge at Rocherath-Krinkelt. Of course, the Bulge was fought in many areas, but it was won for the First Army on this shoulder. The best endorsement of this statement comes from Baron Hasso von Manteuffel, Commanding General of the *Fifth Panzer Army* on the central front, who stated after the operation: 'We failed because our right flank near Monschau ran its head against a wall.' Another endorsement is evident in the telegram from General Courtney H. Hodges, Commanding General of the First US Army, to the Commanding General of the 'Indianhead Division' on 20 December 1944. 'What the Second Infantry Division has done in the last four days will live forever in the history of the United States Army.'

As historians have discovered, Hitler assigned the main effort to the *Sixth Panzer Army* on the north flank under the command of *Generaloberst* Sepp Dietrich and allocated the preponderance of his best troops to this effort – the elite of the *Waffen-SS*. Four powerful Panzer Divisions and five Infantry Divisions included the *12th SS Panzer Division 'Hitler Jugend'*, *12th Volksgrenadier Division* and the *277th Volksgrenadier Division*. All three were involved in the attack on Rocherath-Krinkelt. The mission of this army was to attack through Losheim, roll over the Elsenborn Ridge and on to Antwerp. Some were elite troops, well trained, and employed in an area where success was vital to Hitler's strategy. Obviously, they failed due to the heroic stand of US forces on the north shoulder.

The author of this version of the battle, William C.C. Cavanagh, has probed into every possible source for factual information. He has studied official after-action reports, histories and unit reports of organizations involved in the battle. In addition, he has conducted an extensive program of individual contacts, not only with US Army participants, local villagers and resistance fighters, but also with German commanders at various levels in the three divisions involved in the attack. Such an ample and widespread research effort has enabled the author to separate fact from fiction.

This book tells a courageous story of men who believed in their heritage, and who, through their heroic teamwork and dedication, stopped the main effort of *Sixth Panzer Army*. American veterans who participated in this battle will remember the events, even after forty years, as only yesterday. They will also remember their compatriots and friends who died in this battle. Shakespeare expressed a pertinent philosophy so well in his *King Henry V*:

> *We would not die in that man's company that fears his fellowship to die with us... He that outlives this day, and comes home safe will stand a tip-toe when this day is named...but we in it shall be remembered; we few, we happy few, we band of brothers, for he today that sheds his blood with me shall be my brother.*

The Battle of the Bulge was not fought solely at Bastogne. Here in the northern sector of the Ardennes, elements of tragedy, heroism and self-sacrifice exerted a great influence upon the result of German intentions.

Battles are won in the hearts of the men, not only by the combinations of fire and movement, but also by working together. Teamwork is decisive, as was shown in the northern part of the Ardennes.

General der Panzertruppen
Hasso von Manteuffel
former Commander
Fifth Panzer Army in a taped message to the author, June 1974

Acknowledgements

My search for information on the battle brought me into contact with hundreds of people on both sides of the Atlantic. I therefore extend my sincere thanks to all whose cooperation made this work possible.

My particular thanks to the following people:

First and foremost, my wife Denise and our grown-up children, whose encouragement and patience over the years are a constant source of inspiration for me.

The late Charles B. MacDonald, my close friend and mentor, at whose suggestion I undertook this project. Himself a veteran of this action as a Company Commander with the US 2nd Infantry Division, as well as a prolific author of military history, he went to considerable lengths to help me with my research.

Colonel Charles W. Stockell and the late General Frank T. Mildren, who kindly checked and commented upon the manuscript.

The late Harry S. Arnold, for telling me 'How it was' for a front line rifleman.

Roger V. Foehringer, the late Richard H. Byers and the late Rex W. Whitehead for their true and valued friendship over the years.

Claude E. Norman who left no stone unturned in his efforts to locate veterans of his battalion.

Colonel and Mrs Tom C. Morris for their friendship and encouragement over the years.

The following people all helped in one way or another:

Mr Ray Baranouskas, Mr Keith Bell, Mr Ralph G. Bennett, Colonel Carlo Biggio, Mr George Bodnar, Dr Lyle J. Bouck, Mr Robert W. Bricker, Mr Neil Brown, Colonel George D. Callaway, Major General John H. Chiles, Mr Charles E. Curley, Colonel James W. Decker, Colonel Joseph W. Dougherty, Colonel Robert H. Douglas, Herr Paul Drösch, Frau Hedwig Josten-Drösch, Mr Pierre Dullier, Mr Peter Eden, Mr Louis D. Ernst, Mr Phil Fitts, Colonel John A. Frye, Brigadier General E.F. Graham Jr., Mr Nelson W. Hall, Colonel William F. Hancock, Colonel Holland W. Hankel, Mr Ralph G. Hill, Major General John H. Hinds, Mr Keith Holyman, Major Herbert P. Hunt, Mr Ed Jordan, CSM Joseph E. Keirn, Mr Henry H. Kimberly, Mr William P. Kirkbride, Colonel Matt F.C. Konop, *Obersturmbannführer* Richard Schulze-Kossens, Colonel Eugene A. Lash,

Oberstleutnant Gerhard Lemcke, Judge Harlow F. Lennon, Colonel Samuel Lombardo, Colonel James W. Love, Colonel James F. McKinley Jr., Mr Bernard Macay, Colonel Alexander J. Mackenzie, Colonel George K. Maertens, Mr Michael Mason, Mr Harold R. Mayer, Mr Ron Mayer, Mr Bill Meyer, Colonel Walter T. Michau, Mr Ben Nawrocki, Mr Bob Newbrough, Mr Claude E. Norman, Mrs John C. Oakes, Mr Kendal M. Ogilvie, *Oberstleutnant* Wilhelm Osterhold, Frau Thekla Palm, Mr Harry C. Parker, Mr Robert Parker, Mr Don Rader, Mr Kraig Rice, Colonel Edward C. Rollings, Mr Brian Rowe, Mr Harold Schaefer, Herr Joseph Schroeder, Mr Frank J. Smollom Jr., Colonel Donald H. Smith, Mr Carl Sosna, Colonel Ralph V. Steele, Mr Paul Stevenson, Colonel John H. Stokes, Mr Malcolm Stothard, Mr Delbert J. Stumpf, Mr Leonard Trimpe, Mr William Vacha, Reverend Allyn K. Wadleigh, Mr Byron O. Wilkins, General Wilhelm Viebig, *Oberst* Horst *Freiherr* von Wangenheim, Mr Lee F. Wilhelm, Major General Ralph W. Zwicker.

Introduction

By the late Charles B. Macdonald,
author of *Company Commander* and *A Time for Trumpets:
The untold story of the Battle of the Bulge.*

In late summer of 1944, the dictator of Nazi Germany and self-styled Führer, Adolf Hitler, faced almost certain defeat. In the east, Russian armies were at the Vistula River across from the Polish capital of Warsaw and almost on the frontier of East Prussia. In Italy, Allied armies were approaching the Po valley not far from the southern frontier of what Hitler called the Third Reich. In France and Belgium, having dealt the Germans a serious defeat in Normandy, Allied armies were fast closing in on Germany's western frontier, not far from the Ruhr industrial region, whose mines, smelters and factories were vital to the German war effort.

In the face of those drives, to stand beleaguered on the defensive was to Hitler to assure eventual defeat. In his mind, he had no choice but to go over to the offensive, to strike a decisive blow that would reverse the disastrous course of events; change everything.

To Hitler, the Russian hordes and the vast distances afforded no chance for a decisive blow in the east. Nor would a heavy blow in Italy bring more than local advantage. That left only the Western Front.

On 16 Sepember, Hitler surprised his senior officers with word of what he had in mind. 'I have made a momentous decision,' he said. 'I shall go over to the offensive, that is to say' – he slapped one hand down on a map that lay across his desk, indicating the Ardennes region of eastern Belgium and northern Luxembourg – 'Here, out of the Ardennes, with the objective Antwerp!'

Stunned, Hitler's senior officers saw no hope of the offensive succeeding, but they had to admit – however grudgingly – that the plan was a stroke of genius. After assembling under the cloak of inclement weather that is common in north-western Europe in late fall and early winter, three German armies were to push through the Ardennes, cross the sprawling Meuse River, and drive to the port of Antwerp, thereby trapping four Allied armies north of the penetration. With those armies eliminated – the Canadian First, British Second, and American First and Ninth, more than half the Allied strength – Hitler believed he could convince the Western Allies to settle for a separate peace and then turn all Germany's strength against the Russians.

Convinced that Germany lacked the means for such a grand offensive, the

Commander-in-Chief in the west, Field Marshal Gerd von Runstedt, and other senior commanders tried to convince their Führer to scale down his ambitions, to settle for a limited objective attack to eliminate American forces in the vicinity of the border city of Aachen, the forces posing the most direct threat to the Ruhr industrial region. Yet Hitler refused to listen. Only an offensive on a grand scale, he maintained, would be sufficient to compel the Allies to accept a separate peace.

As preparations got underway, Hitler devised a clever deception scheme. There was to be no mention of the offensive in any message, whether sent by telephone, telegraph, or radio, and everybody let in on the plan, including clerks and typists, had to sign a pledge of secrecy upon pain of death. All preparations were to be pointed towards the Germans launching a major counter-attack north of the Ardennes once the Allies in the vicinity of Aachen had launched an anticipated offensive toward the Ruhr. In the north Hitler paraded the assembly of his panzer divisions before the eager eyes of Allied intelligence. Only over the last three nights before the offensive began were the tanks to shift to the region opposite the Ardennes, the heavily wooded Eifel.

As Hitler anticipated, Allied intelligence officers nibbled hungrily at the bait. Convinced that the Germans were beaten, that they could muster insufficient strength for a major offensive, Allied intelligence officers and their commanders considered that such a capable, professional soldier as von Runstedt would surely use his limited resources sanely and rationally to counter-attack once the Allied offensive began. Although there were some indications that the Germans might be planning a blow in the Ardennes – including a number of intercepted radio messages (known as ULTRA) – Allied intelligence officers saw no strategic objectives in the Ardennes. An attack there would be stupid, and Field Marshal von Runstedt was not a stupid man.

1. Oberstgruppenfuhrer der Waffen SS Josef Sepp Dietrich, commanding general Sixth Panzer Army. (American Document Center, Berlin)

As finally devised, the *Sixth Panzer Army*, commanded by an old political crony of the Führer, *Oberstgruppenführer* Josef 'Sepp' Dietrich, was to make the main effort, employing four *SS Panzer* divisions. Attacking in the northern reaches of the Ardennes, the *Waffen-SS* were to drive swiftly for the Meuse River just upstream from the Belgian city of Liege, which was an American supply base.

In the center, the *Fifth Panzer Army* under *General der Panzertruppen* Hasso von Manteuffel was to push through the Belgian road centers of St Vith and Bastogne and then drive for the Meuse in the vicinity of a big bend in the river at the city of Namur. On the south, a weaker force, the *Seventh Army* under *General der Panzertruppen* Erich Brandenberger, was to protect the southern flank of the penetration.

In view of the heavy losses over six long years of war, the force that the Germans assembled was remarkably strong. There were to be 250,000 men in the first wave and an eventual twice that number. There were to be twenty-eight divisions, including eight armored divisions, plus three separate brigades. Tanks and self-propelled assault guns numbered just over 2,100. Artillery pieces and rocket launchers totalled more than 2,500, but the Luftwaffe was hard put to muster as many as 1,000 aircraft. The Germans were also short – almost cripplingly short – of motor vehicles, and even though there was sufficient gasoline to support the offensive, there might be problems in getting it forward. So, too, perhaps as many as half the German troops were inexperienced, many of them hastily converted sailors and Luftwaffe ground troops, who had received only a modicum of training in ground combat.

As Hitler anticipated, the Americans held the Ardennes lightly. Because the Ardennes – Eifel is hardly conducive under normal circumstances to an offensive, the Allied commander, General Dwight D. Eisenhower, accepted reduced numbers there in order to concentrate on offensives north and south of the Ardennes. When the Germans began their offensive, there would be only four infantry divisions, and elements of light cavalry in the line with an armored division in reserve and a fifth infantry division making a limited objective attack through the lines of the infantry division that was holding the northern end of the line. That meant that at the start of the drive, the Germans would have a numerical advantage of 250,000 to 83,000 and a vast numerical superiority in artillery and tanks.

Along the German frontier, the Ardennes region extends for approximately eighty miles from the vicinity of a picturesque German medieval town, Monschau, south to the vicinity of Echternach, another picturesque medieval town in Luxembourg. Shaped much like an isosceles triangle, it extends westward some sixty miles to the Meuse River. A westward extension of the high plateau of the Eifel, the Ardennes has been so deeply etched through the centuries by serpentine streams that it appears to be less like a plateau than mountains and presents a rugged face scarred by deep gorges and twisting stream valleys. Confined by the escarpments, gorges and dense forest – most of it coniferous – the road net was also serpentine, and although extensive, most of the roads were narrow and poorly surfaced.

For the main effort in the north, the *Sixth Panzer Army* was by far the strongest of the three German armies. Dietrich had three corps headquarters, five parachute and infantry divisions (called *Volksgrenadier* – People's Infantry – an honorific designed to boost morale) four *SS Panzer* divisions (with attached separate tank and assault gun battalions, 800 tanks and assault guns) and more artillery and rocket battalions than the *Fifth* and *Seventh* Armies combined; a thousand pieces.

With two *Volksgrenadier* divisions the *LXVII Corps* was to attack on both sides of Monschau to get onto a high ridgeline inside Belgium, the Hautes Fagnes, meaning High Marshes. There, with the assistance of a battalion of paratroopers, the divisions were to block the limited road net astride the ridge to prevent American reinforcements from moving south from the vicinity of Aachen. Meanwhile, south of Monschau, after a parachute and two *Volksgrenadier* divisions had achieved penetration, two *SS Panzer* divisions of the *1st SS Panzerkorps* were to make the main thrust in the vicinity of two Belgian border villages, Krinkelt and Rocherath, that lie so close together that American troops called them the 'Twin Villages'. Two more *SS Panzer* divisions under another *SS Panzerkorps* were to constitute a second wave.

2. Major General Walter E. Lauer, commanding general 99th Infantry Division.
(Photo: 99th Archives)

However essential good roads were to swift advance by the German armor, the road net in the vicinity of Krinkelt – Rocherath was limited, but the German planners designated five as adequate. Two emerged from a relatively open sector lying between Krinkelt-Rocherath and the road center of St Vith, known as the Losheim Gap, whence German forces had debouched with marked success in 1914 and 1940. The other three, in the vicinity of the twin villages, crossed a broad expanse of high ground that the Americans called the Elsenborn Ridge, the highest ground in the area.

German intelligence was fully aware of the weakness of the American defenses in the north. On either side of Monschau there was only a squadron of mechanized cavalry, and the only division in the line, the untried 99th Infantry Division, held positions extending from the village of Höfen, near Monschau, to the northern

3. Lieutenant Karl W. Volk of the 393rd Regimental Headquarters sporting a captured German war souvenir in Krinkelt.
(99th Archives)

reaches of the Losheim Gap, a distance of twenty-one miles. (Infantry divisions normally defended no more than ten miles.) Only two cavalry squadrons were available for defending the Losheim Gap.

Commanded by Major General Walter E. Lauer, the 99th Infantry Division had entered the line in early November. Like most divisions arriving in Europe in the fall of 1944, the 99th had relinquished many of its trained soldiers as replacements, then shortly before sailing, filled its ranks with men transferred from service units and the Army Specialized Training Program (ASTP), a program designed originally to provide specialist training for men with high IQs. There was little time to train those men in the rigors of ground combat, but General Lauer ordered that once in the line, units were to gain experience through extensive patrolling.

Except at Höfen, a hilltop village affording excellent fields of fire over open slopes, the positions of the 99th Division were inside dense coniferous forests, and in between there were great-undefended gaps, through which German patrols moved at will.

What German intelligence did not know was that another division had moved in behind the 99th. This was the veteran 2nd Infantry Division, commanded by Major General Walter M. Robertson. In early December 1944 the 2nd had been defending the high ground east of St Vith and known as the Schnee Eifel. It relinquished that high ground on 10 December and moved to Camp Elsenborn in preparation for an attack towards the Roer dams. This attack was to be made up the road and through the forest north of Krinkelt and Rocherath.

In the seemingly unlikely event of a German attack from the east, the Germans might be in a position to cut the 2nd Division main supply route other than on foot; a single dirt road led westwood from Krinkelt via Wirtzfeld to the Elsenborn Ridge.

Acutely conscious of the danger facing the 2nd Division, early on General Robertson ordered his engineers to begin work to improve that track. Yet that would only alleviate Robertson's problem, not solve it, for there were trails through the dense forest east of Krinkelt – Rocherath by means of which the Germans might get into the Twin Villages, and if that happened,

4. Major General Clarence Huebner presents the silver star to Major General Walter M. Robertson. (US Army photograph)

the track through Wirtzfeld would be blocked.

There were other roads farther south – one leading west from a frontier crossroads known as Losheimergraben and a north – south road marking the 99th Division's front line and the German frontier which American troops called the International Highway, the other leading from the frontier village of Lanzerath at the northern extremity of the Losheim Gap – either or both of which the Germans might use to cut the 2nd Division's main supply route at Büllingen and proceed on to Krinkelt-Rocherath.

To the U.S. V Corps commander, General Gerow, the possibility that the Germans might counter-attack to cut the 2nd Division main supply route appeared disturbingly real. There were reports of two panzer divisions in the vicinity of the Roer River Dams, which might well react to the 2nd Division's attack by counter-attack. That prompted Gerow to designate a fall-back position should it be required: The Elsenborn Ridge.

In an effort to achieve surprise, the 2nd Division conducted no patrolling before men of its leading regiment, the 9th Infantry, began to march north of Krinkelt-Rocherath into the dense forest soon after daylight on 13 December 1944. Although there was at first no sign of the enemy, the going proved slow, for an early winter storm had dumped more than six inches of snow and in warming weather great globs of snow fell from the pines onto the men below, drenching their wool uniforms.

Some fifty yards from the Wahlerscheid pillboxes, the timber cover ran out, but a thick fog prevented the defending Germans from detecting the approaching force. Under concealment of the fog, a patrol from Company G led by Technical Sergeant Clyde A. Dugan crawled under several bands of barbed wire to reach a communications trench running between two of the pillboxes, but hardly had Dugan's men reached the trench when the fog suddenly lifted. Spotting a German soldier, one man opened fire with his Browning Automatic Rifle (BAR). That gave the patrol away, and withering German fire rained down. Dugan's men could neither advance nor withdraw.

Under covering fire from Dugan and his men, two staff sergeants, James R. Dunn and Adam C. Revera, managed to cut a small path through the barbed wire and joined the men in the trench, but nobody else could get through. Only after nightfall did the men make their way out.

5. A soldier of the 38th Infantry digs in east of the Wahlerscheid road during the 2nd Division attack towards Heartbreak Crossroads.
(US Army photograph)

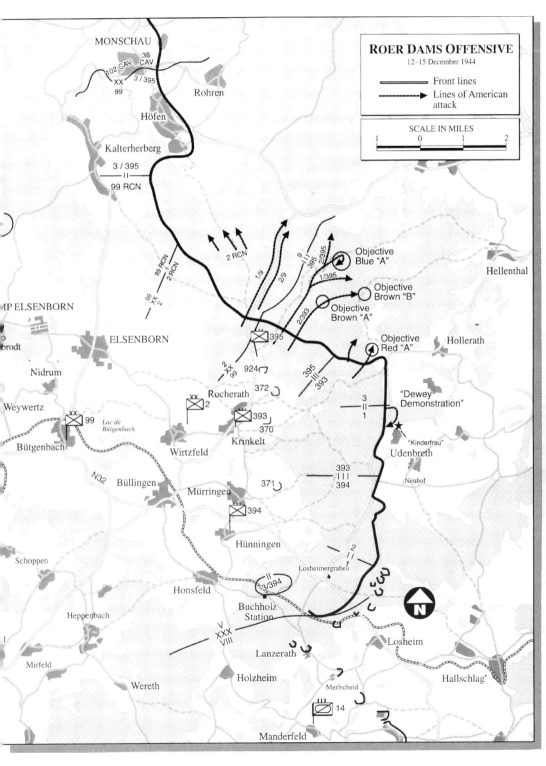

MONSCHAU

102 CAV
38 CAV
XX 3 / 395
99

Rohren

Höfen

Kalterherberg

3 / 395
II
99 RCN

ROER DAMS OFFENSIVE
12–15 December 1944

Front lines

Lines of American attack

SCALE IN MILES
1   0   1   2

2 RCN

99 RCN
2 RCN

1/9
2/9
9 395
III
2/395

Objective Blue "A"

Hellenthal

1/395

MP ELSENBORN

brodt

ELSENBORN

XX 99
2

2/393

Objective Brown "B"

Objective Brown "A"

395 III 393

Objective Red "A"

Hollerath

Nidrum

XX 99
2
924

Weywertz

XX 99
Lac de Bütgenbach

Rocherath   372

XX 2

395 III 393

"Dewey Demonstration"

Bütgenbach

393
370

Krinkelt

3 II 1

"Kinderfrau"

N32   Büllingen

Wirtzfeld

Udenbreth

Mürringen

371

393 III 394

Neuhof

XX 394

Hünningen

Schoppen

Losheimergraben

2 II 1

Honsfeld

II 1/3/394

Buchholz Station

N

Heppenbach

V XXX VIII

Lanzerath

Losheim

Mirfeld

Holzheim

Merlscheid

Hallschlag

Wereth

14

Manderfeld

All through the days of 14 and 15 December, despite a heavy rain of shells fired by 2nd Division artillery, German fire from the pillboxes turned back every attempt by the men of the 9th Infantry to take Wahlerscheid. As darkness came on 15 December, the 2nd Battalion commander, Lieutenant Colonel Walter M. Higgins Jr., learning of the success of Dugan's patrol on the first day, decided to try to exploit the little gap that sergeants Dunn and Revera had cut in the barbed wire. Guided by one of the men who had gained the communications trench the first day, a squad equipped with a sound powered telephone moved silently through the gap. Around 9:30 p.m., the patrol leader, Sergeant Marvin C. Hardy, whispered into the telephone. His men had surrounded a pillbox and the Germans seemed unaware of their presence.

That was all Higgins needed. Within minutes, first one company then another was plodding along single file, following a band of white tape through the gap in the wire. When another battalion quickly followed, the assault began. The men moved swiftly, killing or capturing the occupants of the pillboxes, prodding sleepy Germans from their foxholes. With Wahlerscheid at last in hand, a second regiment, Colonel Francis Boos' 38th Infantry, was soon moving forward to exploit the breach.

Even as the 2nd Division's attack progressed, German troops, tanks and artillery were moving stealthily through the Eifel toward the frontiers of Belgium and Luxembourg all the way from Monschau to Echternach. Parachute and *Volksgrenadier* divisions advanced at first no closer than twelve miles from the front, then moved forward over the last two nights before the jump off day: 16 December. In recognition of the noise created

6. *Five German graves of men killed in the American attack against Wahlerscheid.*
   (Courtesy Tom C. Morris)

7. *The Wahlerscheid Crossroads after the battle.* (*US Army photograph*)

by tanks, the restraining line for Panzer divisions was farther to the rear, but on the last two nights, tanks and artillery pressed even closer to the front over roads spread with straw to muffle the sound of their movement, while planes flew over American positions in an attempt to conceal the noise.

As American troops in their foxholes went about their accustomed routine, unaware of what was about to hit them, the German troops learned for the first time what they were to do. After reading inspirational messages from the army and army group commanders, officers concluded with a call to arms from Field Marshal Gerd von Runstedt.

> *Soldiers of the West Front, your great hour has arrived!! Large attacking armies have started against the Anglo-Americans. I do not have to tell you anything more than that. You feel it yourself.* **WE GAMBLE EVERYTHING!** *You carry with you the holy obligation to give everything to achieve things beyond human possibilities for our Fatherland and our Führer!*

Chapter One

99th Infantry Division

13-16 December 1944

In conjunction with the 2nd Division attack on Wahlerscheid, Colonel Alexander J. Mackenzie's 395th Regimental Combat Team began its own attack towards the German pillboxes on the west bank of the Olef Creek. The attack began at 08:30 on 13 December in dense fog with visibility restricted to 150 yards. As the 395th Combat Team moved forward, units of the 393rd and 394th Infantry staged their own demonstration in support so as to give the impression of an attack along the whole of the division front.

Company B, 393rd Infantry commanded by Captain Henry B. Jones launched one such diversionary attack (referred to as a 'Dewey Demonstration'). At 07:30, Lieutenant Joseph A. Carnevale's 2nd Platoon attacked east across the International Highway just south of Ramscheid.

They were under orders to move as quickly as possible, not to stop to pick up the wounded and they moved smoothly and trouble free to their first three objectives. At their fourth objective they ran into trouble when they hit a mined and booby-trapped area and came under German artillery, mortar and machine-gun fire, which according to Technical Sergeant Ben Nawrocki, seemed to be 'sensing them out'. Casualties mounted as shells and mines detonated all around

8. Lieutenant Joseph A. Carnevale of 2nd Platoon Company B, 393rd Infantry talking to Major General Walter E. Lauer, his division commander, in November 1944.
(99th Division Archives)

9. Sergeant Ben Nawrocki of Company B, 393rd Infantry. (Courtesy Ben Nawrocki)

the platoon. Sergeant Nawrocki later recalled,

Guys would come to me and tell me they were wounded. Then I could hear a lot of others screaming that they were hit. A shell fragment hit Lieutenant Carnevale in the back. I started to push on and when I noticed him, he told me to get the others out first and leave him there. I said 'Bullshit, Sir!' and got him the hell out of there with another guy.

Nawrocki and his men evacuated twenty wounded, and one man, Private George Terrent, was killed in action. The Dewey Demonstration cost Company B dearly.

Colonel Mackenzie's 395th Regimental Combat Team had moved north-east of Rocherath in columns of battalions. Lieutenant Colonel Charles J. Hendricks' 1st Battalion led on the west (left) side of the Hasselpat Trail with the 2nd Battalion under Major Alfred Stevens echeloned to the right rear and Lieutenant Colonel Ernest C. Peters 3rd Battalion, 393rd Infantry abreast of Stevens. The men hand carried all equipment and moved some 3,000 yards without encountering enemy resistance. As the men of Captain Hugh M. Gettys' Company B reached their first objective, a cluster of enemy pillboxes on a hill known as the Wiesenhardt, they came under artillery and mortar fire. Machine gunners in three of the pillboxes opened fire pinning down the attackers whose olive drab uniforms contrasted sharply with the snow. German machine-gun fire killed Captain Gettys as he tried to lead his men in the attack. First Lieutenant Virgil E. Smith assumed command of Company B and as dusk began to fall withdrew his men across the Wies creek and prepared to resume the attack the following morning.

Major Stevens' 2nd Battalion had likewise moved forward but had made

10. Colonel Alexander J. Mackenzie, commander of the 395th Regimental Combat Team of the 99th Infantry Division. (Courtesy Alexander J. Mackenzie)

no significant contact with the enemy. To their south, Colonel Peters' 2nd Battalion, 393rd Infantry had reached its first objective, a stream known as the Olef Creek. Thus far their only difficulty was the rugged terrain, which quickly tired the over-burdened men. At this point, they checked their equipment and, at 11:00, moved towards the next objective, a junction of trails protected by enemy pillboxes.

Captain Donald P. Driscoll's Company E was in the lead with 2nd Lieutenant Edward P. Mann's 2nd Platoon up front. When they first went on line the men of Company E were convinced the war was all but finished. Rumor had it that if they met enemy troops, the Germans would surrender after the first few bursts of fire. Deep down, Private First Class Harry S. Arnold and his buddies suspected that the enemy had no intention of accommodating such a relaxed theory. As the platoon came within sight of the objective, Captain Driscoll pulled back his scouts and kept his men several hundred yards inside the woods, while he informed Lieutenant Colonel Peters.

At about 16:00, Peters came up front and joined Driscoll to evaluate the situation. As they conferred, the enemy spotted them and opened fire with mortars and machine guns, wounding five men in the process. Peters pulled back the battalion a short distance, where they dug in to resume their attack the next morning.

Private Harry S. Arnold spent the night behind a pile of logs in the center of a firebreak. He was never to make that mistake again, since the log pile received much attention all night from a nearby pillbox and its supporting weapons. As he huddled behind the logs, Arnold thought about the rumor that the Germans would surrender and later remarked 'The enemy had not been informed of his role in this farce!'

11. Private First Class Harry S. Arnold of 2nd Platoon, Company E, 393rd Infantry. (Courtesy Harry S. Arnold)

On 14 December, the 395th RCT saw no action of any significance, although it attacked several bunkers with varying degrees of success. Since the 2nd Division was held up at Wahlerscheid, 99th Division headquarters ordered Mackenzie to hold up his advance and dig in for the night.

The next day the 'no advance' situation persisted although attacks against the pillboxes continued. In one such attack Arnold lost his foxhole buddy, a man called Whiting. As medics carried him away on a stretcher Whiting gave Arnold the then famous Churchill twin finger sign.

Throughout the day a continuous stream of wounded men wound its way back to the rear. Captain Bill Smith of Company G, 393rd Infantry had a narrow escape as he stood behind a tree watching a German sentry near a pillbox some twenty-two yards distant. Suddenly Smith heard three sharp cracks and upon looking above his head saw three bullet holes in the tree trunk. He dived to the ground as a fourth shot rang out, wounding one of his men, a Sergeant Standridge. As the medics evacuated him Standridge commented to Smith,'Twenty three years of telling those guys to keep their butts down and the first thing I do is get hit in the ass!'

The 395th RCT spent the remainder of the day consolidating positions captured during the previous two days.

Chapter Two

99th Infantry Division

15 December 1944

In the area around Höfen, Lieutenant McClernand Butler's 3rd Battalion, 395th Infantry occupied a series of open rolling hills with, on its left, Lieutenant Colonel Robert E. O'Brien's 38th Cavalry Reconnaissance Squadron and to its right the 99th Reconnaissance Troop. The attacking elements of the 2nd Division were next in line facing the Wahlerscheid crossroads. The 395th RCT resumed the 99th Division frontage, succeeded in turn to the south by its 393rd and 394th Infantry Regiments. The southernmost element of the 99th Division was the Intelligence and Reconnaissance Platoon of the 394th Infantry. First Lieutenant Lyle J. Bouck commanded this small unit. It held positions atop a wooded hill overlooking the sleepy village of Lanzerath and the Losheim Gap. Aware of the sensitive nature of this sector, General Lauer, the 99th Division commanding general, placed his division reserve, the 3rd Battalion, 394th Infantry, around Buchholz Station, a couple of kilometers slightly northwest of Lanzerath.

Colonel Don Riley's 394th Infantry held a front stretching from a point on the International Highway three miles north of Losheimergraben, south as far as the Buchholz-Losheim railroad. Practically the entire line lay within the forest belt and a two-mile gap existed between the regiment and its southern neighbor, the 14th Cavalry Group. Lieutenant Bouck's I and R Platoon provided the tenuous link between the division and the cavalry to the southeast.

The I and R Platoon had taken over a series of dugouts prepared earlier by

12. Lieutenant Lyle J. Bouck of the I and R Platoon, 394th Infantry on a war bonds drive after the war.
(Courtesy Lyle J. Bouck)

elements of the 2nd Infantry Division while in position on the Schnee Eifel. As a small lightly armed force, they weren't expected to defend their position in the unlikely event of an enemy attack. Their mission was to act as a warning post to the 394th Infantry should the enemy attack out of the Losheim Gap. From their holes at the edge of the trees, Lieutenant Bouck's men had good fields of fire across the road, which ran through the village. A few hundred yards north of Lanzerath, a junction led west to Buchholz then on to Honsfeld. The road between Lanzerath and Losheimergraben was rendered useless due to a demolished railroad bridge.

In Lanzerath itself, the 2nd Platoon of Company A, 820th Tank Destroyer Battalion with four towed 30-inch guns had the mission of maintaining a counterintelligence screen across the sector. Reinforced by twenty men of the unit's 2nd Recon Platoon mounted in an armored halftrack and two jeeps, they were to repulse small raiding parties or patrols. In the unlikely event of a major enemy counter-attack, they were to give warning and resist to the limit of their ability without impairing the integrity of their force. A few civilians remained in the village tending cattle and going about their daily chores. Sany Schur and her parents were only too pleased to offer their liberators what hospitality they could. As the cavalrymen went about their duties, Sany and her mother passed jugs of hot cocoa to them through an open window overlooking the garden. Most evenings, a few soldiers would join the Schur family in a game of cards, after which they would return to their outposts.

Fate had decided that the 394th Infantry was sitting across three roads designated as attack routes by the *1st SS Panzerkorps*. The first of these was a trail leading west from the International Highway (Reichstasse 265) near Udenbreth then through the dense forest to Mürringen and labeled Rollbahn B. The second was the Losheimergraben to Bütgenbach road (N32) referred to on German maps as Rollbahn 'C'. The third was the minor road running from Lanzerath, through Buchholz, Möderscheid and Faymonville and labeled Rollbahn 'D' by the German planners. *Obersturmbannführer* Jochen Peiper's *1st SS Panzer Regiment* would take this road but initial penetration of the American line was to be made by units on loan to the *1st SS Panzerkorps*. One such unit was *Oberst* Wilhelm Viebig's *277th Volksgrenadier Division* facing the 393rd Infantry along the International Highway. Sepp Dietrich would not commit his armoured units to the

13. *Oberst Wilhelm Viebig, commander of the 277th Volksgrenadier Division. (Courtesy Wilhelm Viebig)*

PLANNED ATTACK ROUTES
of the
I. SS-PANZER-KORPS

The precise routes of Rollbahn A, B and C were established from a
battlemap carried by a member of Grenadier Regiment 989 who was
captured by Sgt. George L. Mahnke, 370th Field Artillery Battalion.

Courtesy of the 99th Infantry Division Association

attack until the *277th* and its running mates had penetrated the American
line. *Oberst* Viebig's mission was to protect Rollbahn 'C' against any
American attacks from the north. The *277th* must capture Krinkelt-
Rocherath to prevent American forces using these villages to cut Rollbahn
'C' at Büllingen. Two other German divisions were to open up Rollbahns
'C' and 'D' for the armored advance. *Generalmajor* Gerhard Engel's *12th
Volksgrenadier Division* at the center of the *1st SS Panzerkorps* had Rollbahn
'C' as its main objective, once it had captured the vital road junction of

Losheimergraben just north of Lanzerath. When the *12th Volksgrenadier Division* had secured the road, it was to defend the south flank of *6th Panzer Army*. *Generalmajor* Walther Wadehn's *3rd Fallschirmjager Division* was responsible for the capture of Rollbahn 'D'.

Generalmajor Gerhard Engel's 12th *Volksgrenadier Division* had made its way west under cover of darkness. Walking through the snow their thoughts turned to Christmas. Passing silently through small villages on the German side of the line, here and there they caught sight of the shadow of a villager crossing the deserted street. Now and again, a thin beam of light shone through drawn blackout curtains. No one spoke, the marching grenadiers thought of loved ones back home as they trod through the snow, wary of what lay in store.

Pioneer Helmut Stiegler, an eighteen-year old engineer with the 3rd *Kompanie, 12th Pioneer Abteilung,* of *12th Volksgrenadier Division* and his buddies received an evening meal of sweet rice and plums to be washed down with a mouthful of schnapps. After the meal yet another movement order arrived. During the march to the forward assembly area, Stiegler and his buddies passed men of other units, some in snowsuits, which suggested to Stiegler that they must have been approaching the front line. Eventually, Stiegler's company found accommodation in one of the Westwall concrete bunkers. Throughout the night paratroopers passed by in what was the assembly phase of the coming offensive. Stiegler remarked that, like him, most of the passing soldiers looked young and inexperienced. In the early hours of 16 December, Stiegler's unit moved out to remove a tank barrier. They had to finish their work before dawn and his platoon leader sent Stiegler to get some tape primer to blow up iron girders blocking the road.

Elsewhere behind the German lines, Karl Ziak, an interrogations officer with *Oberst* Viebig's *277th Volksgrenadier Division*, received a movement order. His detachment was to move to Neuhaus, a small hamlet two and a half miles east of Udenbreth. Ziak and his driver, an Austrian named Plemeli, set off for their new location. They found the roads packed with tanks, trucks, artillery pieces and *Nebelwerfer* rocket batteries. To either side of the road, men sat clustered around small camouflaged fires warming their hands, their supply horses tethered to nearby trees. Ziak felt safe from enemy observation since dense, low-hanging clouds covered the entire area.

Upon reaching his destination, Ziak moved into the westernmost house. To his surprise and delight an advance party of motorcyclists and an officer had prepared the house for his arrival. The house was well lit, had a telephone, and the advance party had swept it clean. Above all this however, Ziak's new command post possessed the most prized trophy of all, a wood-burning stove! In the adjoining room men of his detachment lay on the straw covered floor nervously awaiting the start of the coming attack.

To the west, GIs of the 394th Infantry were beginning to feel the lack of such items as galoshes and raincoats. Prior to 16 December, the 2nd Battalion made numerous requests to reconnoiter a possible withdrawal route, should the need arise. The battalion executive officer, Major Ben W. Legare, felt that since the regiment held such a wide frontage, plans for such an eventuality should be prepared. No such plan ever saw the light of day. Prior to 16 December, it emerged that command at the top of the battalion was inept to say the least. The battalion commander never accompanied visiting officers on inspection unless ordered to do so. When questioned about his unit's situation and plans, he was often unable to give a satisfactory reply. As a result, Major Legare and the company commanders lacked confidence in their commander and were unable to concentrate upon their own jobs within the battalion.

To the south near Lanzerath, Lieutenant Bouck felt uneasy in his dugout

atop the Schirmbusch. Over the past few nights he and his men had heard the sound of vehicles moving in the direction of Losheim. Bouck had placed his platoon on alert and the men took it in turn to snatch a couple of hours sleep.

In the early hours of 16 December, *Oberst* Viebig's men made their final move to their forward assembly area. They were to cross the International Highway, clear the forest, then capture the Twin Villages. *Oberst* Horst, *Freiherr* von Wangenheim, Viebig's chief of staff knew well from experience gained in Russia that clearing the forest was a crucial step in the forthcoming attack. Viebig's *Volksgrenadiers* were to advance through the forest on Rollbahns 'A' and 'B', both of which led west through the woods. Rollbahn 'A' led to the Twin Villages and over the Elsenborn Ridge while Rollbahn 'B' led to the Elsenborn Ridge via Mürringen.

14. Oberst Horst von Wangenheim, Chief of Staff of the 277th Volksgrenadier Division. (Courtesy Horst von Wangenheim)

Chapter Three

Armageddon

16 December 1944

At 05:30 on 16 December, a murderous barrage of mortar, artillery and dreaded *Nebelwerfer* rockets exploded the length of the 99th Division front lines. Fortunately for them, General Lauer's infantrymen had improved their dugouts with overhead log cover, so casualties in this initial barrage were relatively light. The incoming fire did however wreak havoc with their communications wire lines both tree-strung and ground laid.

East of the International Highway, Helmut Stiegler and his engineer buddies were on their way back to their unit when the shelling began. To the rear of the German lines, the sky was lit up as German infantry assault formations stumbled west past Stiegler, through the concrete 'dragon teeth' of the Westwall. Upon reaching his unit the young engineer looked west as shells screamed overhead, and felt glad that for once, he and his friends were not on the receiving end.

In its log covered position above Lanzerath, the I and R Platoon sat out the barrage as it moved west towards Buchholz. Down below in the dingy cow town, the Schur family sought shelter in their basement and when the shelling died down, Sany Schur crept up the cellar steps to see what was happening. She entered the kitchen and looking out of the window, couldn't believe her eyes. There was no sign of the American tank destroyer crews who'd received an order to relocate to Manderfeld. Outside, an eerie glow permeated the dense fog as the Germans bounced searchlight beams off the low-hanging clouds. Sany returned to the cellar to tell her parents what she'd seen. Her ageing father replied: 'I fear the worst; the Germans may be coming back'.

In his dugout on the hill, Lieutenant Bouck awaited the expected enemy attack he felt sure would follow the shelling. Much to his surprise, no such attack occurred so he called regiment to report his situation. Regiment ordered him to send a patrol down into Lanzerath and report its findings as soon as possible. Taking three men with him, Bouck set off towards the Buchholz road where he turned right and followed the ditch down into Lanzerath.

Down in the village, a forward observation party from Battery C of the 371st Field Artillery Battalion had moved to the upper story of a house on

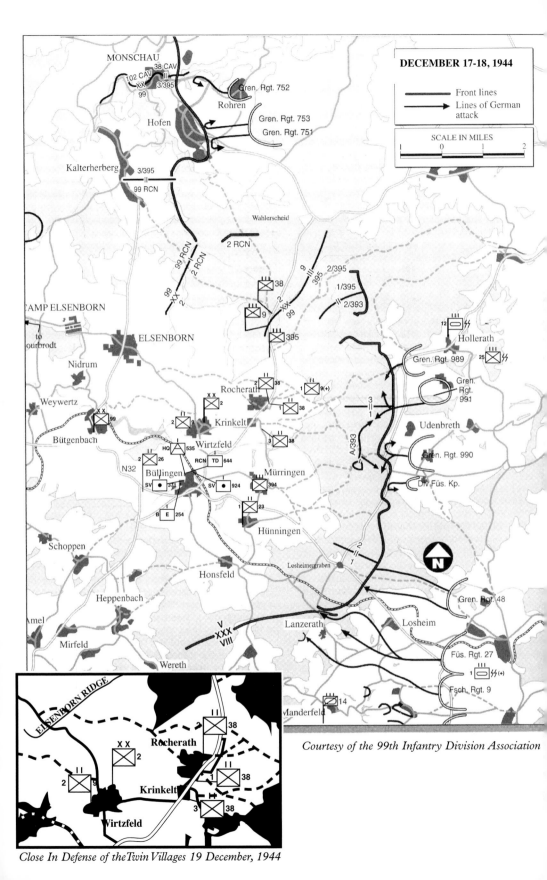

DECEMBER 17-18, 1944

Front lines
Lines of German attack

SCALE IN MILES

MONSCHAU

102 CAV
99
38 CAV
3/395
Gren. Rgt. 752
Rohren
Hofen
Gren. Rgt. 753
Gren. Rgt. 751

Kalterherberg
3/395
99 RCN

Wahlerscheid

99 RCN
2 RCN

2 RCN

9
395
2/395
1/395
2/393

38
9
99
2
A/393
12 ⚡
Hollerath
25 ⚡

CAMP ELSENBORN

to
ourbrodt
ELSENBORN

Nidrum

Weywertz

Bütgenbach

Schoppen

395

Gren. Rgt. 989

Gren. Rgt. 991

Rocherath
2 38
1 9(+)
1 38
Krinkelt
2 9
3 38
Wirtzfeld
HQ 535
RCN TD 644
2 26
Büllingen
SV 371
SV 924
B E 254

Mürringen
394

Hünningen
1 23

3 ⚡
1

Udenbreth

Gren. Rgt. 990

Div Füs. Kp.

99
2

N32

Honsfeld

Losheimergraben

2
1

N

Gren. Rgt. 48

Heppenbach

Amel

Mirfeld

Wereth

V
XXX
VIII

Lanzerath

Manderfeld
14

Losheim

Füs. Rgt. 27
1 ⚡ (+)

Fsch. Rgt. 9

Courtesy of the 99th Infantry Division Association

ELSENBORN RIDGE

XX
2

Rocherath
38

2 9

Krinkelt
1 38

Wirtzfeld
3 38

Close In Defense of the Twin Villages 19 December, 1944

15. Lieutenant Warren P. Springer of Battery C, 371st Field Artillery Battalion whose observation party joined the I and R Platoon 394th Infantry in its position at the edge of the trees in the Schirmbusch overlooking Lanzerath. (Courtesy Warren P. Springer)

the east side of the street where they established an observation post. The party consisted of Lieutenant Warren P. Springer, his instrument sergeant Peter A. Gacki, Corporal Billy S. Queen and Corporal Willard Wibben. Looking down the street to the southwest, they spotted a long column of enemy soldiers heading in their direction. Lieutenant Springer, a short stocky ex-Massachusetts state trooper, decided to pull back towards Buchholz so he and his men climbed aboard their jeep and headed for the rear.

Meanwhile Lieutenant Bouck and his three men had entered another house, which had been used by the tank destroyer men who had pulled out for Manderfeld as soon as the barrage stopped. Bouck and his men went upstairs to get a good view down over the valley. Upon opening a bedroom door, they surprised a man in civilian clothes talking over the telephone. One of the Americans, Private William Tsakanikas, pulled out his bayonet and ordered the man to raise his hands. Aware of the impending arrival of enemy troops, Lieutenant Bouck decided they couldn't risk killing their prisoner and ordered Tsakanikas to let the man go. From this upstairs window, the four Americans spotted the approaching German column. Bouck ordered two of his men, Technical Sergeant William Slape and Private John Cregar, to remain in the house and observe the road. He told them to return to the platoon position once the Germans reached the

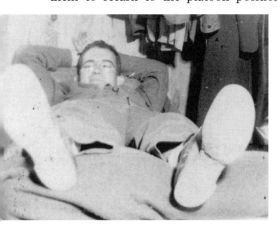

outskirts of the village. Bouck and Tsakanikas went back up to the platoon position and not long after their arrival, Lieutenant Springer and his men joined the I and R Platoon in its defense of the Schirmbusch.

16. Corporal Billie S. Queen of Battery C, 371st Field Artillery Battalion, the only man killed in the I and R Platoon action atop the Schirmbusch. (Richard H. Byers)

Fearing that Slape and Cregar might end up trapped in the village, three other men, Corporal Aubrey McGhee, Private Jim Silvola and Private 'Pop' Robinson, volunteered to go down and bring back their buddies. Cautiously, they set off down the Buchholz road towards Lanzerath. Unfortunately, just as they left the position, Slape and Cregar set out back to the position via a more direct route.

In his foxhole at the edge of the trees, Lieutenant Bouck could hardly believe his eyes. A column of enemy soldiers who Bouck recognized as paratroopers, was marching up both sides of the road into the village. Unknown to Bouck and his men, these were men of the *3rd Parachute Division's 9th Infantry Regiment*. Such units with battle honors including Eben-Emael and Monte Cassino under their belts had, by December 1944, been assigned the role of regular infantry. Few veterans were left in the division and many rear echelon officers commanded elements of the division. The advancing column reached the first houses in Lanzerath.

In their cellar, the Schur family decided to risk a trip upstairs and into their kitchen. As she sat drinking coffee, Sany heard the sound of hob-nailed boots, and a male voice swearing in German in the barn next door. She stood up and opened the door to find a German paratrooper smashing a US field telephone to pieces. When he saw the girl, the soldier entered the kitchen, looked around, and then walked out without saying a word. The war the Schur family had thought was over, had come back to Lanzerath.

At the edge of the trees, Bouck's men held their fire as about 100 enemy soldiers passed directly below the platoon position. A few yards behind the column, a separate group of three men, whom Bouck presumed to be the

17. *A message sent by the I and R Platoon 394th Infantry at 16:03 on 16 December 1944 to say that they were still holding their position. (99th Division Archives)*

From Danzig:

    At 1550 report from I and R outpost: We are holding our position. Enemy strenght 75. They are moving from .anzerath d to railroad. We still are receiving enemy arty fire. Ammo OK.

            rec'd at 1603
                        GW

Hq	CG	393 Inf	Ren Tr	Spec Staff	
Journal	Asst CG	394 Inf	Sig Co	Corp	
Workshop	C of S	395 Inf	Or Co		
D O	G-1	Div Arty	Q. Co		
Evaluation	G-3 ✓	324 Engr	Hq Co		
	G-4	324 ,c	CIS		

1603

unit commander and his staff, were walking up the road. The I and R Platoon held their fire until most of the enemy column was within range.

Suddenly a curious thing occurred which took away Bouck's chances of surprising the Germans. A young blonde haired girl ran up to the trio of enemy officers and pointed excitedly up to the I and R position. An NCO barked an order and the paratroopers dived into the roadside ditches on either side of the road. The girl ran back to the nearest house and a firefight broke out, during which the Germans attempted a frontal attack up the hill,

18. Major Robert L. Kriz, Intelligence Officer of the 394th Infantry of the 99th Division. (Courtesy Robert L. Kriz)

which afforded no cover. The I and R Platoon opened fire stopping this attack and killing several Germans. Lieutenant Bouck called his regimental command post in an attempt to get artillery support. He spoke with Major Robert L. Kriz, the regimental S-2 (Intelligence Officer) who told him that no artillery was available but that he and his men should 'Hold at all costs'.

A loud crack told Bouck that a bullet had shattered his radio. Lieutenant Springer had better luck than Bouck in that he managed to bring down a few rounds before enemy fire put his radio out of action.

Down below the position and in the trees just north of the Germans, Corporal McGhee and Privates Silvola and Robinson, decided to re-join the platoon. They made a break to cross the road but came under heavy small -

arms fire, which forced them back into the trees. After several such attempts, they realized the futility of their action, and set off north hoping to join the 1st Battalion, 394th Infantry north of the railroad cutting.

At about noon, the Germans evacuated some of their wounded from the slope under cover of a white flag. Moments later, they renewed the attack, by which time the defenders were getting low on ammunition and realized they couldn't hold on much longer. Bouck's men gritted their teeth and prepared for the worst.

North of the I and R Platoon, the Germans had attacked the 394th Infantry's 1st and 2nd Battalions in strength on 16 December. At about 07:35, men of the 2nd Battalion, spotted German infantry moving from the east through the mist and dense undergrowth in front of their position. In this sector, prior planning by the Heavy Weapons Company Commander and the Artillery Liaison officer paid off. Artillery fire pounded the attacking troops (a fusilier company of the *990th Regiment* of the *277th Volksgrenadier Division)* and succeeded in driving them off.

A short while later, the Fusiliers, supported by three tanks, resumed their attack towards the International Highway, along the road from Neuhof. Under a smokescreen, the tanks moved towards Company G. At this point, Technical Sergeant Fred Wallace called artillery down on his own position, effectively stopping the German attack, and the tanks turned back towards Neuhof. The defenders killed or captured all German infantrymen remaining in the Company G area. Overhead log cover on the dugouts protected Wallace and his men as artillery rounds exploded all around them. The Germans made their main attacks against the 393rd Infantry to the north, and in the center and right flank of the 394th Infantry further south.

All attacks in the 393rd/394th sector were aimed at punching holes through the US front line so that the armored columns of the *Leibstandarte 1st SS Panzer Division*, and those of the *Hitlerjugend 12th SS Panzer Division* could best exploit Rollbahns 'A', 'B', 'C' and 'D' in their dash to the Meuse River. Between Losheim and Losheimergraben, the Germans had destroyed a road bridge that crossed the railroad track, during their retreat in the fall. Likewise, they had destroyed a bridge over the deep railroad cutting between Lanzerath and Losheimergraben. The approach to Losheimergraben, whether from Losheim or Lanzerath, was denied to all but infantry, until the railroad itself could be captured and the bridges repaired.

As soon as the early morning barrage lifted, soldiers of the 1st and 3rd Battalions 394th Infantry emerged relatively unscathed from their foxholes. Lieutenant Colonel Robert H. Douglas, commanding the 1st Battalion, set out to inspect his front-line companies in order to determine how they had fared during the shelling. Company A under Lieutenant Willard S. Clark, was on the battalion right between the railroad and the Losheim-

Losheimergraben Crossroads
1st Battalion/394 vs 48th Volksgrenadier Regiment

(1) A Co/394 bivouac area. [Trees logged after battle.]
(2) South flank of B Co/394 area. C Co beyond.
(3) D Co/394 Mortars.
(4) D Co/394 Mortar Platoon Command Post.
(5) D Co/394 Mortar's second withdrawal position area.
(6) B Co Sgts Hilliard and Trent occupy house with their platoons and fight from windows.
(7) B Co survivors emerge from draw followed by Volksgrenadiers.
(8) General direction of attacks by 48th Volksgrenadier Regt/12th Volksgrenadier Division.
(9) House used by CN Co/394, A Btry/371 and C Btry/371 forward observation parties prior to attack. First house occupied by Germans ffrom which Major Osterhold shouted surrender terms.

(10) Houses occupied as fall-back fighting positions by Anti-Tank Co/394 and remnants of 1st Bn/394 before surrendering to Maj. Osterhold.
(11) German assault gun knocked out with bazooka from house by Sgts Weidner and Kirkbride.
(12) Cannon Co/394 gun position.
(13) International Highway between Belgium (E) and Germany (W) to Lanzerath (S) and Hollerath (N).
(14) Rollbahn 'C' to Losheim (E) and Bullingen (W).
(15) Road to Buchholz and 3rd Bn/394 area.
(16) Chateau Buffalo Bill.
(17) Temporary German cemetery with some American bodies.

Losheimergraben road, overlooking Losheim. Captain Sidney A. Gooch's Company B occupied the battalion center front with its right flank tied into Company A and astride the Losheim to Losheimergraben highway. Captain James Graham's Company C occupied the left of the battalion front with its left flank tied in to Company G of the 2nd Battalion. Colonel Douglas reached the Company C position and asked Captain Graham what he had done during the shelling. Graham, a big Texan, replied,

> *Hell, Colonel, I just stayed here under cover till it was over; wasn't any use getting my head blown off.*

Colonel Douglas resumed his inspection of the battalion position. Three 57-mm anti-tank guns protected the road leading into Losheimergraben from Losheim. Heavy machine guns of Company D were in position supporting Companies A and B. The 81-mm Mortar Platoon was dug in about 200 yards south-east of the Losheimergraben crossroads. Men of the platoon used a couple of wooden huts just south of the crossroads for shelter.

The Company D mortars were located in a clearing among very tall trees to the east side of the road leading south of the crossroads. Lieutenant Bill Vacha, a forward observer with the platoon, was in the command post when the barrage hit the position. A shell burst filled the building with flying chunks of metal, wounding Corporal George E. Bero. Lieutenant Vacha and other men tried in vain, to stem the flow of blood from Bero's wound but he died within minutes. Realizing how vulnerable they were, the remaining six men went down into the cellar for protection against the incoming shells.

19. Lieutenant Bill Vacha of Company D, 394th Infantry at Losheimergraben. (Courtesy Bill Vacha)

When the shelling stopped, Vacha set off towards the mortar emplacements where he was pleased to find that not a single casualty had occurred. There had been considerable damage to equipment with two jeeps and trailers damaged beyond repair. By daylight, the mortar men had restored communications and the platoon awaited instructions on fire missions Vacha returned to the command post. To the south, in the direction of Lanzerath, a raging firefight could be heard. *Volksgrenadiers* of *Oberstleutnant* Wilhelm Osterhold's *48th Grenadier Regiment, 12th Volksgrenadier Division*, were attacking the Company A position. Numerous obstacles stood in their way – fallen trees, mines, and barbed wire all combined with disorientation to slow them down. South of the *48th*, *Oberstleutnant* Georg Lemms' *27th Fusilier Regiment* attacked over more open country leading directly to the railroad line.

Approaching the railroad cutting, after their unsuccessful attempt to re-join the I

20. Oberstleutnant Wilhelm Osterhold of Grenadier Regiment 48, 12th Volksgrenadier Division. (Courtesy Wilhelm Osterhold)

and R Platoon, Silvola, Robinson and McGhee took it in turns to carry a Browning automatic rifle, as they ploughed through the dense undergrowth. When they reached the deep railroad cutting, the three men slid down the incline onto the track, and then clambered up the other side. Reaching the top, they entered the trees and immediately came under heavy small-arms fire. Silvola looked around, to find that German soldiers surrounded him and his two buddies. A Short firefight ensued but the Americans soon ran out of ammunition. Silvola reached towards his belt for another clip, only to find he had none left. Lemm's fusiliers realized what was happening and came out in the open, weapons at the ready. Without thinking, Silvola sank to his knees, hands raised above his head in surrender. An enemy soldier made the Americans stand together then went through their pockets. From Silvola's pockets he took a knife and two old coins, and then sent his prisoners down the railroad under guard towards Losheim and several months of captivity.

Generalmajor Engel, commanding the *12th Volksgrenadier Division*, kept *Oberstleutnant* Gerhard Lemcke's *89th Grenadier Regiment* in reserve as his other two regiments pressed home their attacks on Losheimergraben. An American jeep, driven by Germans, made a reconnaissance of the Losheim to Losheimergraben road. It sped off back down the road and returned a few minutes later leading a *Sturmgeschutz* assault gun. As the *Sturmgeschutz* approached one of the American anti-tank guns, the gun crew fired, knocking off a track. The second shot, penetrated the hull and a third set the vehicle on fire. The crew bailed out and the men of Company B knocked out the jeep with small-arms fire.

Immediately following this incident, several things started almost simultaneously. Large numbers of German infantry began moving west along the railroad. The 99th Division lost contact with the 14th Cavalry Group. A German combat patrol of about 175 men penetrated the area due west of Company A using the railroad cutting as access. Soldiers of the 3rd Battalion, 394th at Buchholz, deflected this patrol which then fell back to attack the Company A command post. Initially, Company A repulsed this attack and Lieutenant Clark's men hit the enemy flank driving them into the Company D mortar position.

The mortar men were well aware that this German force was on its way. Lieutenant Vacha and Lieutenant Marion L. McQuarry decided to check on their men. They set out on foot intending to circle the position in opposite directions. As the officers approached each other, a German soldier fired at them with a 'burp gun' (MP-40 *Schmeisser* machine pistol). McQuarry fell forward, mortally wounded and Vacha hit the ground as his men opened fire with their carbines on the advancing Germans.

The Germans took cover and the mortar platoon commander decided to call for artillery support. His section leaders told him they would rather use their mortars, so he agreed to their request. Section Sergeant Delbert J. Stumpf yelled at his men to turn their 'tubes' around. Due to the close proximity of the enemy, Sergeant Stumpf realized he must act quickly. He ordered his men to prop the bipod legs of their mortars up on the edge of their emplacements so as to fire at an angle of about 89 degrees. They then reduced the range at which their rounds would fall by removing all powder increments from the rounds, and using only the shotgun-type propellant. Stumpf wanted his rounds to detonate close to him and his men, as quickly as possible, since the nearest German was by then only fifteen yards away. He gave the order to fire as he reported back to the platoon commander by telephone.

21. Sergeant Delbert J. Stumpf of the Mortar Platoon Company D, 394th Infantry. (Courtesy Mildred Stumpf)

Private First Class Bob Newbrough, a rifleman with Company D, sat crouched in his slit trench adjusting fire as the mortar shells, many of them tree bursts, rained down on the enemy soldiers, some five yards distant. Newbrough actually felt comfortable. Having gone through intensive training with these mortar crews, he had every confidence in their ability. The Germans withdrew, leaving several dead behind and Vacha's men took two prisoners whom they sent back to the platoon command post for interrogation.

Back at the 1st Battalion command post, his men brought Colonel Douglas one of the first German prisoners. The man was a small medic, about five feet six inches tall and wearing a helmet that was far too big for him. Having studied a little German at school, Colonel Douglas decided to try and make use of it. Raising himself to his full six feet one, he thundered

'Wie heissen sie, Dumkopf?' The German medic looked at Douglas and in excellent English replied, 'I am sorry sir, I don't understand a word you say. By the way, I have a cousin, Hans Schmidt. He lives in Milwaukee; do you know him?' That ended the Colonel's demonstration of his ability in German rather abruptly.

Major Norman A. Moore's 3rd Battalion, 394th Infantry based around Buchholz station acted as 99th Division reserve. Company I under Captain J.J. Morris, plus a machine-gun detachment from Company L, were acting in support of the 393rd Infantry. This left the 3rd Battalion slightly under strength with about 735 men. Headquarters Company was located at Buchholz Station while Company L, under Lieutenant Neil Brown, was directly to the east and on both sides of the railroad with the company command post in the station itself. Captain Wesley K. Simmons' Company K and Captain Joseph M. Shanks' Company M occupied positions on both sides of a road leading from the station to a junction with Rollbahn 'C' about 750 yards west of Losheimergraben.

During the early morning barrage, an unfortunate incident occurred at this road junction. An anti-tank gun (unit unknown) had been in position there for over a week. The crew had not taken the trouble to dig any sort of dugout. As German shells began falling in the area, the two gunners abandoned their gun and started running wildly for any cover they might find. In their impulsive search for safety, they ran blindly into positions occupied by the 3rd Platoon of Company K. Oblivious to the numerous verbal challenges issued, they tore the cover off one of the Company K foxholes. The occupants opened fire, killing one of the gunners instantly and critically wounding the other.

Just before 08:00, men in the 3rd Battalion sector around Buchholz Station were awaiting the arrival of their mess truck from the rear. As they stood waiting in the cold morning air, several men of Company L spotted movement to the southeast along the railroad track. Initially, they presumed this to be the men of their 4th Platoon coming in to eat a warm breakfast. It then occurred to the men standing that something was wrong. Company L always took breakfast in platoon order, starting with the 1st Platoon. They issued the customary challenge and ordered the advancing strangers to halt. The man in the lead of the group gave a command in German and his men began deployment on the north side of the railroad. In an account he sent the author, First Lieutenant Neil Brown, commanding Company L, 394th Infantry at Buchholz Station, recalled his memories of that December morning:

> *Later the same morning, at exactly 0705 (by both wrist watches I carried) I looked out of the window down-track from Buchholz Station, and noticed soldiers walking alongside of the track. Our chow line had just been set up behind the station and some of the soldiers from the platoon that was behind the building were in line about to eat. Because I knew that Sergeant Klug had set up a schedule for each of the platoons to walk to the station to be fed, instead of carrying food to the platoons, upon seeing these soldiers coming down either side of the railroad tracks, I turned to Klug and said 'Klug, that 1st Platoon is coming in for breakfast. What the hell is going on?' Klug came alongside me by the window and peering down that railroad track, he said to me - at about the same time it was also clear to me- '1st Platoon my ass, those are Germans!' With no hesitation, and with no direction, Klug grabbed his carbine, which he had hung from the wall to our backs, inside the station. He ran out the door to the left, around the station and headed down the track on a dead high run.*
>
> *Elmer Klug was a regular army enlisted man from East Peoria, Illinois. He had enlisted during the worldwide economic depression of the 1930s when employment in the US was very hard to find and had worked himself*

up to a staff sergeant's position by the time a cadre was
selected from the 7th Infantry Division for the newly
activated 99th. He came to Company L as a first sergeant
and never served in any other company that I know of. He
was an enormous man, near six feet tall, a superb athlete,
barrel-chested, bull-necked with cauliflower ears from
professional wrestling, an avid baseball fan, and every way
that I knew a first class soldier. He was a perfect gentleman
and knew more about managing soldiers than I ever learned.

Klug ran as hard as he could down that railroad track
towards the approaching Germans. I watched this entire
procedure while talking to battalion on the telephone. When
Klug got within about 50 or 70 yards from the lead
Germans, in a voice that I could clearly hear inside the
station, he yelled a thunderous 'HALT!' Believe me, every
one of those Germans stopped. I watched the third German,
in my right hand column, turn and start yelling out orders to
the others. Klug shot him in the back and dropped him cold.
Klug turned, crouched and ran back towards the station and
upon entering, told me that in his judgment, there were
between twenty-five and fifty in this group. He wasn't quite
sure, because they had scattered after he shot the one barking
out orders to the others. Some of the Germans got into a
couple of empty railroad cars that were on a siding in the
station yard, and at least one, climbed to the top of a nearby
water tower. Klug then left the station and went around to
where the mess line was set up. He told them to pack up the
chow line and get it out of there. He then mustered the
platoon that was preparing to eat into service along the left

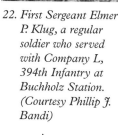

22. First Sergeant Elmer
P. Klug, a regular
soldier who served
with Company L,
394th Infantry at
Buchholz Station.
(Courtesy Phillip J.
Bandi)

side of the station. At about the same time as the platoon began moving
towards the dispersed Germans, artillery, in great abundance, came down
on the station and the areas to the left and right of it. The glass in the front
end of the building was immediately blown out and automatic weapon fire
came in though the shattered window. I stood up once to look down the
track and a bullet went under the left edge of my helmet, alongside the left
side of my neck before striking the wall behind me.

While Klug was out on his one-man challenge, I had the battalion
headquarters on the line, and told them we had German soldiers in our
area, and that we didn't know how many or where they had come from. I
also said that we were trying to protect ourselves and deal with the
situation. The response from battalion was that I was to keep them
informed. The battalion headquarters soon knew that we had some serious
problems in the vicinity because the artillery fire was also hitting the edge
of the battalion command post location. Major Moore ordered his staff to
put together a perimeter defense around the command post. The artillery cut
communication with battalion but Lieutenant Wesley K. Zuber soon had it
restored. We were still receiving artillery fire in the railroad yard, although

of less intensity than at the outset. Major Moore called to tell me that I was to assemble my company and report to Lieutenant Colonel Douglas in the 1st Battalion area. He had heard from regiment which had been in touch with division headquarters, who said that whatever was going on in my area was nothing but a small patrol; and that the main thrust of the German operation was on the highway in Lieutenant Colonel Douglas' area. Moore had been directed to cause whatever troops he still had under his control to be placed at the discretion of Lieutenant Colonel Douglas to help him.

I heard this message as we were right in the middle of a firefight, and I told Major Moore that we were occupied and that as soon as I could gather up the people and disengage, I would report to Lieutenant Colonel Douglas. In the meantime, the platoon that I had thought was coming in to breakfast too early reported to me that they were out of ammunition. I never found out what they were shooting at. Sergeant Klug told me that he would see what he could do about taking care of the ammunition problem.

A squad from the platoon that had been preparing to eat breakfast behind the station volunteered to carry a supply of ammunition to the left of the railroad tracks and forward to the platoon that told me they were out of supplies. This squad ran by the left corner of the station, dispersed just a few yards apart and carrying ammunition, with some two man loads, an artillery shell burst right in the middle of them, killing some. Among the dead was a young ASTP soldier, who had been fairly successful as a concert pianist before he was transferred out of college into the infantry at Camp Maxey.

Over a period of more than an hour, we received artillery fire in and around the station, punctuated by small arms fire, and a few times by automatic weapons fire. We weren't very effective because we couldn't clearly figure out where the fire was coming from, and if anyone moved around the station, fire from someplace seemed to develop. I know that some German soldiers climbed into two boxcars, and I guess that occasionally some fire was coming from these boxcars. I know that at least one soldier made an attempt to climb into a water tower in the railroad yard, but I'm not sure whether he made it or not. At the time I believed he did.

We had a lot of artillery fire in and around the station and I was of the opinion that it was directed by someone who knew that it was important to keep that railroad station under fire and to minimize movement in and around that building. The artillery fire developed on the station rapidly following the dispersal of the German soldiers by Klug. I thought that someone in that group had called in the fire because they had a good field of observation over the station building.

During these first artillery blasts, a soldier in the command post with me, Bodnar and Klug received a wound to the spine and I thought he was dying. I opened a first aid packet and stuffed a bandage into the wound while trying to figure out what battalion was telling me over the phone. It was quite a while before the artillery fire settled down enough for us to move that man away from the front of the station, around the back from where they later evacuated him.

Sergeant John B. Claypool and Technician Fifth Grade George F. Bodnar had overheard me yelling that we had to do something about getting those Germans out of the boxcars and that man off the water tower or we'd all be killed by artillery fire. I believed that a German in one of those two places was directing the fire on the station area. Bodnar went around the station and came in from the south side of the building. He fired a bazooka twice, but both shots missed the boxcars. Claypool later went around and repeated the maneuver several times until no more bazooka shells were available, all of this without effect on the boxcars or water tower.

Elmer Klug was aware of the bazooka fiasco, and he asked me if I had any objection to turning Staff Sergeant Savino Travalini loose on the boxcars and the water tower. They had known each other a long time, and since Travalini was in our area, and theoretically under our control as part of the intended division reserve, I, of course, had no objection. In no time, Klug had the arrangements made, how I'm not sure, to get Travalini in there. Travalini and two other soldiers, with a jeep and an antitank gun, rolled up from the rear and south of the station. He methodically turned the jeep around and unhooked the gun, totally oblivious of any danger from his exposed position. He prepared the gun for firing, and then fired several direct hits into the boxcars and at least one into the water tower, then hitched up the gun and pulled away. Throughout this incident, Travalini and his men experienced no form of enemy resistance whatsoever.

Later that morning, during a calmer few moments Sergeant Klug undertook the counting of German dead around the station and organized evacuation of some wounded. He discovered one dead German to be in possession of a leather briefcase containing a copy of an inspirational general field order given to German troops by Field Marshal Gerd von Runstedt. Lieutenant Brown let Klug keep the briefcase and sent the contents to battalion, who passed it on to Major William B. Kempton, the 394th Operations Officer. This turned out to be the first documented proof of German intentions to fall into American hands during what today is referred to as the 'Battle of The Bulge'.

The Americans took about thirty German prisoners in the course of the action that morning. The Germans seemed to be present in considerable numbers so the remaining two platoons of Company K came to reinforce the position.

At about 11:00, an estimated two companies of enemy infantry attacked Company K from the south-east. Being well dug in, the soldiers of Company K put the attackers under a deadly hail of fire. Supported by their 60-mm mortars, after about forty-five minutes they forced the Germans to withdraw. A German machine gun about 400 yards south of the station pinned down men of Sergeant Travalini's anti-tank platoon. The intrepid sergeant crawled up the road and knocked out this gun using a fragmentation grenade. Later in the action, Travalini discovered that the enemy was in a roundhouse about 300 yards south-east of the Company L command post. He fired several bazooka rounds into the roundhouse and, as the enemy soldiers took flight, he picked them off with his M-1 carbine. For his part in this action at Buchholz, he was promoted to 2nd Lieutenant and awarded the Silver Star.

Persistent attacks against the 3rd Battalion indicated the enemy's determination to make a penetration in this area. The Germans made all such attacks along the railroad bed or via the woods east of Buchholz. As yet, no German column had tried to get up the road from Lanzerath to Honsfeld. Thanks to the tenacity with which the I and R Platoon was defending its position, no enemy troops could use the road. At Buchholz Station, it had become clear that the troops there would soon be completely surrounded. No reinforcements were available since all units were engaged elsewhere.

As dusk approached, German paratroopers managed to outflank the I and R Platoon and entered the position. They systematically moved from hole to hole, taking prisoner the occupants. Corporal Billie Queen, one of Lieutenant Springer's men was critically wounded in the stomach while manning a machine gun. A burst of MP40 fire hit William Tsakanikas in the face severely wounding him. Within minutes, the Germans overran the entire position and marched their captives down the hill into Lanzerath. Lieutenant Bouck and a German carried Tsakanikas, whose face was half shot away. The captors forced Gacki and Wibben to carry out a wounded German, while Billie Queen was left for dead. The I and R Platoon and Springer's observation party had fought a crucial action, although they didn't realize it at the time.

At about 16:45, as soon as dusk would permit, a patrol from Company K, 394th went down the Lanzerath road on reconnaissance. Around 18:00, the patrol returned and reported that they had searched the area for about 500 yards without meeting enemy soldiers. They also said they had heard tank movements off to the southeast. Minutes later, the 3rd Battalion received instructions to leave two rifle platoons in defense of Buchholz. The remainder of the battalion under command of Captain Wesley K. Simmons of Company K was attached to the 1st Battalion to reinforce its main line of resistance. Lieutenant Joseph P. Rose of Company K remained at Buchholz in command of the company's 1st and 2nd Platoons as the rest of the battalion moved off to the northeast.

When this move began, the 99th Division artillery battalions, in firing positions north and northeast of Krinkelt-Rocherath came under intense hostile artillery fire. This barrage lasted about three hours and it was obvious that the Germans knew the precise location of each 99th gun battery. Lieutenant Colonel Logan Clarke, commanding the 924th Field

Lanzerath

(1) I&R Platoon dug-in positions 18 inf'tymn plus 4 arty'mn vs 2 battalions of paratroopers [trees logged off after after battle].
(2) Separate bunker with 3 I&R men.
(3) Route of 9th Parachute Regt, 3rd Para Div.
(4) German Gov't refugee house from which little girl ran out to warn paras.
(5) Direction of repeated attacks during the day.
(6) Route and direction of final attack at dusk.
(7) Cafe Palm.
(8) Christophe and Adolph Schur house.
(9) Anna Christen House. C Btry/371 F.A. Bn observation post.
(10) School and A Co/820th Tank Destroyer Bn command post.
(11) 2nd Plt and Recon Plt/A/Co/820th T.D. Bn sleeping quarters..
(12) Scholzen house. I&R/394 observation post.
(13) Cafe Scholzen.
(14) Nicholas and Sany Schugens house.
(15) View of Losheim across valley.
(16) Road used by Kampfgruppe Peiper to Buchholz, Honsfeld, Bullingen.
(17) Road to Losheimergraben.
(18) Sivola, Robinson and McGhee cut off. Try to escape north. Captured by 27th Fusiliers at R.R. cut.

Artillery Battalion, reported no casualties although the shelling played havoc with his men's nerves and eardrums.

Sometime after dark, Lieutenant Harold R. Mayer and two other members of the Survey and Observation section of Battery C, 371st Field Artillery Battalion, pulled into Buchholz station in their jeep. They parked by a barn on the left side of the road (when heading in Honsfeld direction) and just off the sharp bend to the west. Next to the barn and other outbuildings, they entered a stone house, where Sergeant Richard H. Byers went down into the basement with his bedroll. In the darkened cellar, infantrymen of Lieutenant Rose's rearguard ate rations by the light of a single Coleman lantern. Byers went to another section of the basement and spread out his bedroll.

At 21:00, Captain Simmons and his men took up defensive positions about 600 yards north-west of Losheimergraben. Most of the men hadn't eaten since the evening meal of 15 December and they were running low on ammunition. Captain Simmons made a request for re-supply of both but neither was received. It became obvious that the Germans were concentrating for a further push against the 394th. Aware of the regiment's

23. Lieutenant Harold R. Mayer of Battery C, 371st Field Artillery Battalion. (Courtesy Harold R. Mayer)

25. Richard H. Byers received a battlefield commission shortly before being wounded on 5 February 1945 east of Losheimergraben when his jeep struck a mine.
(Courtesy Richard H. Byers)

precarious position, General Lauer asked the 2nd Infantry Division for help. He then informed the 394th commander, Colonel Don Riley, that Lieutenant Colonel John M. Hightower's 1st Battalion, 23rd Infantry was to occupy defensive positions south and southeast of Hünningen.

Around Losheimergraben, the 1st Battalion, 394th re-formed to protect the crossroads. The Company D 81-mm mortar platoon moved to a new position about 700 yards north-west of the crossroads on the north side of the road to Büllingen. From there they could still fire in support of the 1st Battalion troops who were defending Losheimergraben, and at the same time, be less exposed to direct attack against their firing positions.

By 23:30, Colonel Hightower's 1st Battalion, 23rd Infantry was in Büllingen. Here they de-trucked and marched southeast to Hünningen where guides from the 99th led them into positions on the south and southeastern edges of the village. The battalion command post was established in Mürringen, a village about 1,000 yards north of Hünningen.

The 2nd and 3rd Battalions, 23rd Infantry, of the 2nd Division moved into the vicinity of Wirtzfeld and the villages of Krinkelt-Rocherath.

That night, General Robertson and his chief of staff, Colonel Ralph W. Zwicker, prepared a plan of withdrawal from the Wahlerscheid crossroads. General Leonard T. Gerow of V Corps arranged for the 26th Infantry Regiment of the 1st

24. Former Sergeant Richard H. Byers of Battery C, 371st Field Artillery Battalion re-visits Buchholz Station in December 1994. (Author's collection)

Infantry Division to move to the vicinity of Camp Elsenborn. Thus far, the Germans had chosen to ignore the US salient at Wahlerscheid, preferring to concentrate their efforts upon the capture of the Rollbahns.

At midnight, Sergeant Byers left the farmhouse basement at Buchholz and stood guard outside with an infantryman. The two men took it in turns to duck inside the house and have a cigarette. In the distance they could hear the racing of engines and the rattle of tank tracks. Byers remarked that the noise reminded him of that made by a bunch of Quartermaster troops during the Louisiana manoeuvers.

Chapter Four

393rd Infantry Regiment

16 December 1944

Lieutenant Colonel Jean D. Scott's 393rd Infantry Regiment was dug in north of the 2nd Battalion, 394th Infantry at the eastern edge of the forest, just west of the International Highway. Part of Company C was east of the road while the rest was dug in just west of the road. The 393rd was minus its 2nd Battalion under Colonel Peters, which was acting in support of the Roer Dams attack attached to the 395th Regimental Combat Team. Major Mathew L. Legler's 1st Battalion, 393rd was deployed in positions extending from a point just west of Udenbreth, northwards for a distance of about 2,750 yards. Two major gaps existed between the 1st Battalion and its northern neighbor, Lieutenant Colonel Jack G. Allan's 3rd Battalion, 393rd. These gaps could be covered by small-arms fire, but by virtue of necessity, the line was basically a series of strong points punctuated by gaps.

Colonel Allen's 3rd Battalion, occupied positions north of Major Legler's 1st. The 3rd Battalion front line veered off to the west, some one and a half miles due west of Hollerath. The regimental right lay about 120 yards west of the Westwall defenses, whereas its left was more than a half-mile from the German lines. At the point where the 3rd Battalion turned northwest, the International Highway turned due east towards Hollerath. Colonel Allen's command post was situated on the east bank of the Jansbach Creek on the south side of Rollbahn 'A'.

Some 4,500 yards west of the International Highway lay the farming villages of Krinkelt-Rocherath. These two small farming communities stand astride the Wahlerscheid road, at that time the main north-south road through the 99th Division sector. Clustered along the road, the dingy houses were typical of pre-war Belgium. The stone built church was the dominating feature of the villages, with a commanding view over the surrounding

26. Colonel Jean D. Scott (on left) and an unknown officer of the 393rd Infantry inside a dugout on the Elsenborn Ridge. (99th Division Archives)

28. Major Mathew L. Legler,
    commander 1st Battalion, 393rd
    Infantry in the Krinkelterwald.
    (Courtesy Mathew L. Legler)

29. Lieutenant Colonel Jack G. Allen,
    commander 3rd Battalion 393rd
    Infantry. (Courtesy Jack G. Allen)

27. Lieutenant Colonel Ernest C. Peters, commander 2nd Battalion 393rd Infantry atop
    Elsenborn Ridge. (99th Division Archives)

30. A V-1 *flying bomb destroyed this building in Rocherath prior to the battle. (99th Division Archives)*

31. *The 393rd Regimental Command Post in Krinkelt prior to the battle. (99th Division Archives)*

32. *Lieutenant Colonel Thomas H. Griffin, Executive Officer 393rd Infantry standing outside the 393rd Infantry Regimental Command Post in Krinkelt prior to the battle. (99th Division Archives)*

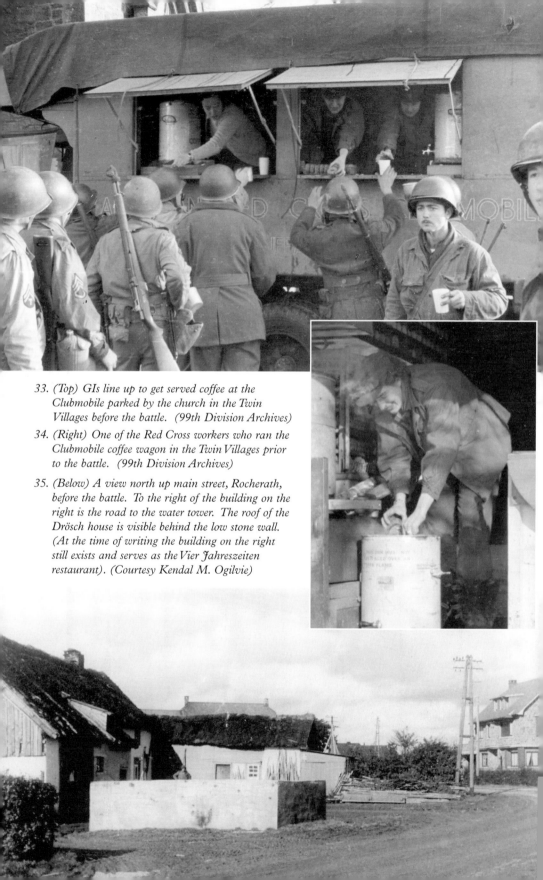

33. (Top) GIs line up to get served coffee at the Clubmobile parked by the church in the Twin Villages before the battle. (99th Division Archives)

34. (Right) One of the Red Cross workers who ran the Clubmobile coffee wagon in the Twin Villages prior to the battle. (99th Division Archives)

35. (Below) A view north up main street, Rocherath, before the battle. To the right of the building on the right is the road to the water tower. The roof of the Drösch house is visible behind the low stone wall. (At the time of writing the building on the right still exists and serves as the Vier Jahreszeiten restaurant). (Courtesy Kendal M. Ogilvie)

countryside. Rollbahn 'A' led from the east through the dense forest across the Olef and Jansbach Creeks and into Rocherath. The villages were of great tactical importance as they commanded the main communications and supply route to both the 2nd Division 'corridor' and the 99th Division front lines.

At 02:00 on 16 December, a patrol from Captain Henry B. Jones' Company B, 393rd Infantry, returned to the company command post. They had turned back, having sighted German troops lying in massed formation along the entire company front. Captain Jones made a call for artillery fire on this area but no such fire materialized. The terrain favored a defense in depth, but the entire *277th Volksgrenadier Division* was about to attack the 393rd Infantry.

36. Krinkelt church as it was in November 1944. (US Army photograph)

As elsewhere, at 05:30, on 16 December the Germans began their attack. Artillery fire, rockets and mortar shells burst on the 393rd positions without pause until 07:00. The barrage completely wrecked the intricate telephone net-

37. A view of Krinkelt from the church steeple. (99th Division Archives)

work and in some cases radio communications also failed.

As soon as the barrage lifted, waves of attacking *Volksgrenadiers*, many wearing snow camouflage, began to charge the 3rd Battalion foxhole line. Staff Sergeant Vernon L. McGarity, a squad leader with Company L, had been slightly wounded by enemy artillery. He went to the battalion aid station for treatment of his wounds, but refused evacuation and returned to his squad.

In his foxhole near the International Highway, Lieutenant Joseph Dougherty of Company K could hear small-arms fire as the Germans attacked the neighboring platoon of Company K and Company B further to the south. Dougherty could not see the attackers but estimated that an entire enemy battalion had attacked Company K. He contacted his company commander and suggested that the 1st Platoon be allowed to withdraw and move to defend the company command post, which

38. First Lieutenant Joseph W. Dougherty of Company K, 393rd Infantry.
(Courtesy Joseph Dougherty)

39. Three soldiers of the 393rd Infantry standing outside the Café Rauw in Krinkelt which the Americans renamed 'The Dead Horse Theatre'. (99th Division Archives)

40. *On the left is Captain Henry B. Jones, Company B, 393rd Infantry Regiment. This company held positions on the west side of the International Highway. (Courtesy Henry. B. Jones)*

faced an immediate threat from its right flank. His suggestion was approved so he led his men to the rear of the command post where their company commander Captain Stephen B. Plume joined them.

A few minutes later, enemy troops attacked the position as they poured through the gap between the 1st and 3rd Battalions. The destruction of his communications prevented Captain Plume from calling for artillery support and soon thereafter the Germans surrounded the remnants of Company K. They managed to penetrate the company foxhole line using Rollbahn 'A' and Plume sent his executive officer and litter squad to the rear, with instructions to give Colonel Allen a report on the situation. The attackers swarmed over the Company K foxholes and Plume lost contact with his platoon commanders. He and Dougherty reached the conclusion that withdrawal would be impossible.

Dougherty could see enemy soldiers moving to the north and at about 08:00, his men ran out of ammunition; they left the position individually in an attempt to reach the battalion command post. Aged twenty-one, Lieutenant Dougherty was aware of the tactical doctrine that forbade unauthorized withdrawal. Fear of a court martial prompted him to stay put.

By 08:55, the 3rd Battalion had restored most of its communications and word of its plight had reached the regimental command post in Krinkelt. The *277th Volksgrenadier Division* had penetrated three quarters of a mile west down Rollbahn 'A'. Colonel Allen, the 3rd Battalion commander, used his reserve platoons in an attempt to try and stem the German tide. At about 09:30, the enemy reached the vicinity of the battalion command post, around which, Companies L and I were then dug in as a last ditch defense. With the assistance of mortar and artillery fire, Allen's men held the enemy at bay, forcing him to detour, so as to continue his advance to the west. Cooks, mortar men and headquarters staff all fought desperately, firing their small arms at very short range and effectively holding off the Germans.

At about 10:00, Lieutenant Dougherty took the decision to surrender and succeeded in arranging a ceasefire. He stood up and began walking towards the Germans, some fifty yards distant. Two enemy soldiers yelled as the young American officer approached them. In his excitement, Dougherty was still carrying his M-1 carbine as he walked forward to surrender. Dropping the weapon, he waved his men forward. For them the war was over. Viebig's *Volksgrenadiers* lined them up and made them carry two wounded Germans down a firebreak to an abandoned US anti-tank gun position.

About fifteen minutes later, in a 'last ditch' defense of his headquarters location, Colonel Allen ordered his companies to close in for an all round defense of the command post area. At 14:00, he received a message telling him that Company I of the 394th Infantry, under Captain J. J. Morris, was on its way from division reserve to reinforce him and his men. Allen sent out guides, who met the reinforcements and brought them into the battalion area at about 16:00. Fortunately, the newcomers brought in a supply of ammunition, and the Germans made no further attempts to attack the position that afternoon or evening.

Early that evening, *Oberst* Viebig's *989th Regiment* reached the east bank of the Olef Creek. They had suffered enormous casualties with many taken prisoner by the 'Amis'. With the onset of darkness, the *989th* could no longer continue its attack and stopped to lick its wounds.

During the day's fighting, the 3rd Battalion radio was out of action, but by nightfall, they had re-established contact with the 370th Field Artillery Battalion. Despite his supply route being cut, Colonel Allen felt optimistic about his men's chances of holding the command post area overnight. At about 19:00, the regiment in Krinkelt ordered Colonel Allen to attack the following morning, and re-capture the Company K position just west of the major bend towards Hollerath in the International Highway.

The battalion had been hit very hard, but despite having had no hot food since the evening of 15 December; the men had fought steadily throughout the day. Only two of the battalion kitchens remained in service, the rest having been overrun. It was not possible for these two kitchen units to supply the whole battalion, so most of the men had to make do with cold 'C' Rations. Some time around 23:00, an American ambulance set off to the rear, carrying several wounded men. On the trail, enemy soldiers stopped the vehicle in the inky darkness. After several minutes of discussion, the Germans agreed to let the ambulance resume its journey to the west. They insisted, however, that they would not let it return to evacuate any more casualties.

*41. American POWs including men of Captain Frederick J. Macintyre's medical
    detachment of 3rd Battalion, 393rd Infantry. (Captured German photograph)*

To the south of the 3rd Battalion, Major Mathew L. Legler's 1st
Battalion, 393rd Infantry, had also been attacked in strength early that
morning of 16 December. Just before the attack, Sergeant Ben Nawrocki of
Company B was in his foxhole in the 2nd Platoon position. He took the
spare pair of socks which he kept tied around his waist and removed his
boots to change socks and rub his frozen feet. He had just changed his socks
and fastened his boots when the German artillery barrage began. He and
his foxhole buddy crouched together to sit out the deadly tree bursts. A
shell-burst extinguished their improvised lamp – a woolen sock stuffed
inside a bottle of gasoline. Outside, tree branches crashed to the ground as
shell fragments tore through the dank forest. When the shelling stopped,
Nawrocki emerged from his shelter and in the artificial moonlight he
spotted enemy soldiers moving slowly through the snowy undergrowth
towards Company B. The Company B position was pock marked with rings
of dirt, where incoming shells of varying caliber had exploded in the snow.
Company B opened fire and the *Volksgrenadiers* dropped like flies. A 2nd
Platoon BAR man piled up the enemy dead like cordwood and Nawrocki
could see that in his haste, the BAR man had forgotten to put on his boots
and was firing the weapon bare-footed.

42. Lieutenant Harry C. Parker, commander Mine Platoon, Anti-tank Company 393rd Infantry led his men in a bayonet charge in support of Company C, 393rd Infantry. (Courtesy Harry C. Parker)

To the right of Company B, Sergeant Lee F. Wilhelm of Company D had not yet made contact with any German attackers. To his north, he could hear the sound of heavy firing in the area of Company B. Likewise to his south, he could hear the sound of gunfire in the Company C position. The sector to his front was blanketed with Company D mortar fire in support of Companies B and C. This fire was of the textbook variety and deterred any German advance towards Wilhelm's position. Throughout this initial attack, his platoon never fired a single shot in anger, simply because they never saw any Germans to fire at.

In keeping with established procedure, half the platoon set off towards the Company C kitchen, where they usually had breakfast. The kitchen lay slightly to the rear, on a footpath parallel to the front line. In the kitchen area, they saw their first Germans, strewn around where tremendous firefights had taken place and were still going on. Wilhelm and his men were surprised at the magnitude of the enemy attack, there they were, in all innocence, carrying their mess gear, and expecting to eat breakfast. All around them men were fighting for their lives. A Company C non-commissioned officer spotted the approaching GIs and yelled at them to get back to their position. Upon their return, they found that all was quiet and resumed their protection of the Company C flank.

Oberst Viebig then decided to throw in his reserves and, by sheer weight of numbers, the Germans managed to penetrate the 1st Battalion front line. By 08:30 the Germans were launching strong attacks against Company C and nearly had the position surrounded. The 1st Platoon of Company B began to fall back. Lieutenant Charles Kingsley sent Sergeant Nawrocki to the company command post to ask for help but none was available. By 10:15 the German on-slaught had engulfed two platoons of Company C. Major Mathew L. Legler, the battalion commander, asked regiment for help. Captain

43. Men of the Mine Platoon, Anti-tank Company 393rd Infantry dig in on the east side of Krinkelt. (Courtesy Harry C. Parker)

George K. Maertens, commanding the regimental anti-tank company, had the only available reserves, in the form of his anti-tank mine platoon. Captain Maertens acted quickly and ordered this platoon, under Lieutenant Harry C. Parker, east of Krinkelt, to establish contact with Company C. In a letter to the author Harry Parker recalled his experiences of that cold December day in 1944:

> *My platoon was the only reserve not on line and we were ordered to counter-attack. As we approached the Company C headquarters (a bunker in the pine forest) we started receiving tree bursts of artillery fire. I observed Germans setting up a machine gun and ordered my men to fix bayonets and charge. The artillery and machine gun fire made it necessary for us to advance as quickly as we could, which we did with a lot of yelling and noise. We killed one German and the others fled quickly. The Company C platoons forward of the command post were killed or captured in the pre-dawn German assault by Germans in snow camouflage uniforms. We joined with Company C and set up a perimeter defense where we spent the night.*

A short distance further north, Sergeant Bernard Macay of the 1st Platoon, Company B, realized that he and a few other men were cut off from the rest of the company. Some twenty yards to Macay's front, across the International Highway, a wounded German soldier lay crying for help. Macay and another man crossed the road and managed to rescue the wounded German. Back in the platoon position, the *Volksgrenadier* became hysterical with fear. It emerged that he believed that the Americans tortured prisoners to death and not too long thereafter, this man died from loss of blood resulting from a serious leg wound. Captain Jones, the Company B commander, withdrew his 2nd and 3rd Platoons to form a perimeter defense of the company command post area. By late afternoon, despite an intense hammering, Major Legler's 1st Battalion still hung on tenaciously to most of its original front-line foxholes. The Germans had penetrated the position but nowhere did Major Legler's men break contact and run.

At the close of the day, Colonel Jean D. Scott's 393rd Infantry still held some of its front-line foxhole line. At one point in the attack, Sergeant Nawrocki of Company B, called supporting artillery down just east of the company command post. This shellfire crept slowly and deliberately eastwards and using their small arms, the Company B 'Dogfaces' held the line. It had taken two entire regiments of the *277th Volksgrenadier Division* all day to infiltrate the foxhole line defended by three American battalions.

Late that afternoon of 16 December, Karl Ziak received word that the first prisoners had arrived in Neuhaus for interrogation. Ziak placed his prisoners in a barn and invited one, an officer, to eat with him and his men. The American seemed surprised that his captors should show kindness towards an enemy. Ziak told him that he could stay the night, provided that he didn't try to escape. The man agreed and, as a precaution against escape, the Germans removed his boots.

The 393rd Infantry could not hope to hold its position much longer. Major Legler's 1st Battalion had lost over half its effective strength. To the north, Colonel Allen's 3rd Battalion had lost over 300 men. In the fast-growing darkness, German soldiers wandered through the dense forest, calling out in English, to catch the tired Americans unaware. Sergeant Wilhelm and the men of Company D could hear activity both to their left and right. They were without radio or telephone and began to wonder if they were doing the right thing in staying put. They still hadn't had contact with the enemy and were not sure what to do. The valiant stand made that day gave the tired remnants of the 1st and 3rd Battalions the breathing space they so badly needed. As the Germans settled down on the west bank of the Olef creek, Lieutenant Colonel Paul V. Tuttle's 3rd Battalion, 23rd Infantry, prepared to move from its position as 2nd Infantry Division reserve to defend the west bank of the Jansbach creek and Rollbahn 'A' leading to the Twin Villages.

Colonel Tuttle had received word of his unit's attachment to the 99th Division early on the afternoon of 16 December. The 3rd Battalion was to move to an assembly area on the western edge of the forest and east of the Twin Villages. This particular spot is called Ruppenvenn and is where Rollbahn 'A' exited the forest. Colonel Tuttle received no other orders except that his battalion was not going to take part in the attack towards the Roer River dams. He set off in advance of his men in order to establish contact with Colonel Scott of the 393rd Infantry at his command post in Krinkelt.

As the 3rd Battalion vehicles rolled through Krinkelt, Major Vern L. Joseph, Colonel Tuttle's Executive Officer, rode at the head of the column in his jeep. Few civilians remained in Krinkelt-Rocherath, the majority having been evacuated on 8 October. Those villagers still present found themselves under the supervision of the US appointed burgomaster, Mr Paul Drösch. They had been allowed to remain in the area in order to tend cattle and other livestock. As Major Joseph rode through Krinkelt, no lights shone from the dingy farmhouses on either side of the main street, each of which sported the customary manure pile outside the front door. In pre-war Belgium, it was said that the wealth of a farmer could be estimated by the size of the manure heap outside of his home.

44. Lieutenant Colonel Paul V. Tuttle of 3rd Battalion 23rd Infantry of the 2nd Infantry Division. (Courtesy Paul V. Tuttle)

To the north and east of the villages, the distant boom of artillery could be heard and fresh shell holes in the snow bore testimony to the ferocity of the early morning barrage. Upon reaching the Baracken crossroads some 800 yards north of Rocherath, the 3rd Battalion convoy turned east towards the distant woods. V-1 flying bombs passed overhead closely followed by a hail of fire from guns of the 535th Anti-Aircraft Automatic Weapons Battalion. At 16:30, the column stopped about 100 yards away from Ruppenvenn where the men de-trucked and lined up on both sides of the narrow road in the mud stained snow. Colonel Tuttle and his operations officer, Captain Morris B. Montgomery, were standing side by side to disperse their men. Captain Montgomery ordered Captain Charles B. MacDonald of Company I, to take his company east on Rollbahn 'A' and establish a roadblock on the west bank of the Jansbach some 600 yards inside the forest. He told MacDonald that the 3rd Battalion, 393rd Infantry, lay someplace between them and the enemy. Colonel Tuttle's orders were to attack to the east and establish contact with Colonel Allen and his men. Captain Montgomery said that he was of the opinion that Colonel Tuttle would try to postpone the attack until the following morning. After all, his men were in unfamiliar territory, carrying only a basic load of ammunition and it was fast becoming dark.

As Company I moved off to the east, incoming artillery and rocket fire obliged Captain Macdonald to take his men east through the woods on the north (left) side of Rollbahn 'A'. Lieutenant Walter J. Eisler's Company L had just cleared Ruppenvenn moving off to the southeast when artillery and rocket fire rained down, killing seven men and wounding twenty. The 3rd Battalion vehicles managed to turn around and returned safely to the Twin Villages.

Lieutenant Eisler positioned Company L about 500 yards south of Ruppenvenn and covering two forest trails, one leading to the southwest, the other to the southeast and Weissserstein. Company K, by then under the command of Lieutenant Lee Smith dug in between Companies I and L but spread out as thinly as they were, the 3rd Battalion companies couldn't tie in effectively with each other, yet no alternative deployment was possible.

Late on the evening of 16 December, Colonel Tuttle informed his company commanders that their planned attack was no longer possible. In view of the magnitude of the German attack, General Robertson ordered Tuttle to stay put and help block the enemy advance towards the Twin Villages. In the darkness, a load of large shovels, pick axes and axes arrived, along with a supply of small-arms ammunition. As yet, however, the 3rd Battalion had no anti-tank mines or bazooka rockets available. Colonel Tuttle called in his company commanders and informed them that Lieutenant Victor L. Miller's 3rd Platoon of Company C, 741st Tank Battalion would arrive in the morning to support them. Two of these tanks were to support Company I while the other three would turn south of Ruppenvenn in support of Company L. Colonel Tuttle's men huddled, frozen in their shallow slit trenches and prepared to do their best to stop the Germans.

Major Thomas S. Bishop, the Assistant Operations officer (G-3) of the 99th Infantry Division kept a diary and that first evening of the German attack he wrote:

> *All hell broke loose today. German army attacked in strength on our right boundary vicinity Honsfeld. 14th Cavalry Command Post on our right flank withdrew 8 miles to our rear and exposed our entire right flank. We are fighting like hell. Situation is obscure but it looks to me like a big push. We are in a very bad situation. We are attacking on our left, and defending on our right. We have identified four German divisions so far today, they have all bounced off.*

Chapter Five

Büllingen Sector

17 December 1944

Having been attacked by a vastly numerically superior force, the 99th Infantry Division was by now unable to put up a cohesive defense. German infantry had penetrated the 99th main line of resistance by exploiting the numerous gaps in the over-extended division front. Individual elements of the 99th Division had put up a good show and German armor would not gain the US rear till these units were destroyed. The failure of the 14th Cavalry Group to hold onto the Losheim Gap had enabled the 3rd *Fallschirmjager Division* to capture Lanzerath. Having taken the I and R Platoon position, the German paratroopers failed to exploit the situation immediately. At midnight on 16 December, *Obersturmbannführer* Jochen Peiper commander of the reinforced *1st SS Panzer Regiment, 1st SS Panzer Division*, arrived at the Café Scholzen in Lanzerath. Upon questioning the paratroop commander about the US units to his front, it emerged that young inexperienced German troops had made a feeble attempt to reconnoiter US positions in the direction of Buchholz Station. All such patrols had seriously overestimated the American strength, given the fact that only Lieutenant Rose's platoon remained there, the rest of the division reserve having been deployed elsewhere.

Peiper, a hardened veteran of the vicious fighting in Russia, immediately seized the initiative, as was his custom. He decided to launch an attack towards Buchholz as soon as possible, using his own regiment as well as the paratroop battalion already in Lanzerath. As Peiper chewed out the paratroop commander, who, incidentally out ranked him, Lieutenant Bouck sat exhausted on the floor of the bar in the Café Scholzen. The young lieutenant had removed a silver identification bracelet and placed it inside one of his boots to prevent the Germans from taking it. As Peiper strode out of the café, a cuckoo clock struck midnight. It was Bouck's twenty-first birthday and beside him, William Tsakanikas, the youngest man in the platoon, lay semi conscious, his combat jacket soaked in blood. In the pre-dawn darkness of 17 December, Peiper's powerful column rolled into Buchholz Station. Lieutenant Rose sent a radio message over his SCR 300 radio to confirm that enemy tanks and infantry were overrunning his position. Leaving the basement, Lieutenant Mayer entered the courtyard only to realize that Byers and Fletcher were still asleep. He ran back down the steps to shake Sergeant Byers out of his sleep and whispered urgently, 'Get up, there's tanks outside!' Byers and Sergeant Fletcher buckled on their pistol belts and rushed up the basement steps following their lieutenant. Outside in the dark courtyard, they paused to pull on their galoshes, and then headed for the back door of a nearby barn. They intended taking the radio from their jeep and using it to call fire down upon the German vehicle column. As they started for the front door of the barn, they saw three German paratroopers coming up the driveway. Standing still, they could see the Germans silhouetted against the white snow. Despite his 6ft 6ins frame, the Germans couldn't see Sergeant Byers with the blackness of the barn to his rear. Since the paratroopers seemed to be armed with MP40 machine pistols and had the backing of an entire armored regiment, the three Americans decided against arguing for possession of the radio. They dashed back to the rear exit of the barn and into the trees to the rear. In the woods, confusion reigned supreme. Infantrymen stumbled blindly through the trees, trying to get away from the road. Fletcher bent down to buckle up his overshoes and when Byers turned around, he was gone, taken prisoner by the Germans. Byers and Lieutenant Mayer made their way to the roadside where they waited till a gap appeared in the German column and raced over the road to the railway track. They followed the railroad then turned north in the direction of Hünningen and could distinctly hear the German column heading for Honsfeld. Peiper's lead vehicles drove into Honsfeld catching the Americans unaware of their newfound predicament. Some tried to resist, but Peiper's SS men and the paratroopers riding his tanks soon overwhelmed them. Among the Americans captured in Honsfeld, were men of Company B, 612th Tank Destroyer Battalion. A group of SS men marched these prisoners into a field and lined them up to be shot. The German who was to carry out the shooting, started down the row of men, firing as he went. Men at the other end of the line made a break for freedom and ran to nearby fields or buildings. Only four made it to safety, one, a sergeant, was wounded by incoming American artillery fire which he nevertheless used as a means of locating the general position of American forces. Hours after the incident, the sergeant, in a state of shock,

45. *Sergeant Luther Symons (on the left) and other soldiers taken prisoner in Honsfeld are marched into Germany under guard through Hasenvenn on 17 December 1944. (Courtesy Luther Symons)*

46. *American GIs killed on main street, Honsfeld in front of the cattle trough.*
(Captured German film)

stumbled into an aid station in Sourbrodt for treatment. After the war, the local Catholic priest, Father Henri Signon, testified that he himself witnessed this incident at Honsfeld and helped bury the victims. The road west of Honsfeld was in poor condition, so Peiper decided to turn north towards Büllingen in order to continue his drive to the Meuse River. This manoeuvre would effectively place him to the rear of Hightower's 1st Battalion, 23rd Infantry in its positions east and southeast of a Hünningen, from where he could advance on Rollbahn 'C' towards Bütgenbach. A variety of American units occupied Büllingen. These included: elements of the 2nd Quartermaster Company, 2nd Divarty Air Section, 99th Divarty Air Section, Service Battery 924th Field Artillery Battalion, elements of the 254th Engineer Combat Battalion, and part of Recon Company, 644th Tank Destroyer Battalion. On the southern edge of Büllingen, men of Captain James W. Cobb's Service Battery, 924th Field Artillery Battalion, under Lieutenant Jack Varner, prepared a roadblock on the road leading south towards Honsfeld. Lieutenant Varner and his men set up their roadblock on the southern end of Büllingen. Varner's platoon comprised a few riflemen, a 30-caliber machine gun, and a bazooka team. Sergeant Grant Yager, accompanied by Privates Arthur Romaker and Santos Maldanado, took up a bazooka position behind a small knoll and facing south. Private Bernard Pappel manned a 30 caliber machine gun slightly off to the bazooka team's left rear and on a fork in the Honsfeld road. Lieutenant Varner and the rest of his men were dispersed along a hedgerow in a field to the right (west) side of the Honsfeld road. As Peiper's lead tank approached the roadblock Sergeant Yager loaded his bazooka only to find that the sight was missing from the weapon. This delayed Yager firing the bazooka

47. *Sergeant Grant Yager of Service Battery, 924th Field Artillery Battalion who disabled Peiper's lead tank on the south edge of Büllingen early on the morning of 17 December 1944. (Courtesy Grant Yager)*

long enough for the first tank to pass down the road towards the village. Yager then fired a rocket at the second tank by simply aiming down the barrel. He fired at a range of thirty-five yards, hitting the side of the tank, which then stopped at the roadside. The escape hatches opened and as the crew baled out, Yager shot the first two men with his carbine. As he fired at the third crewman, the carbine jammed. The rest of the advancing column stopped and *SS Panzergrenadiers* riding halftracks, dismounted in order to attack the roadblock. A Short firefight ensued during which the Germans captured most of Lieutenant Varner's men. Lieutenant Varner and a couple of his men played dead, while the Germans marched the rest of the men to a field on the east side of the road. On their way to this same field, the three bazooka men saw another man from their unit lying wounded alongside his 30-caliber machine gun. They recognized him as Private Bernard Pappel and helped him to the field where the Germans allowed them to tend his wound. The enemy column then continued on its way into Büllingen drawing occasional small-arms fire from either side of the road. The lead tank gunner spotted three Americans and raked the area with machine-gun fire. Before the artillerymen realized what was happening, a tank round burst in their midst wounding Corporal Deloise A. Rapp and Private Paul A. Cusano, but leaving the third man uninjured. Back in the field, an SS officer, wearing a reversible white snow camouflage jacket, ordered Yager and his two buddies onto the hood of an infantry halftrack. He apparently believed the halftrack and its crew would draw less fire in town if they drove in with American POWs on the vehicle. As they climbed onto the halftrack, a single pistol shot rang out in the cold morning air. Romaker, who was sitting behind Yager, exclaimed 'My God, they just shot Pappel in the head!' The same SS officer, who'd permitted them to tend Pappel's head wound had calmly pulled out his pistol and murdered the wounded machine gunner. As the column drove off down the road into the village, Corporal Rapp lay motionless at the roadside where he had fallen, listening to the passing vehicles. Further into town just before the junction with the main street, confusion reigned supreme as the SS men and paratroopers shot their way through town. While most of Service Battery ended up being captured, ten of its soldiers and an officer, First Lieutenant E. Eldon Shamblin managed to escape by the skin of their teeth. They included twenty-year old Staff Sergeant Stuart Boone who many years later wrote an account of his experiences that morning in Büllingen:

> *Service Battery was in Büllingen, Belgium, billeted in local residences. Before bedding down that night (16-17 December) Captain Cobb, our Battery Commander, warned us that we were without much infantry out in front of us. He advised us to dig foxholes in the yards, for our protection, if needed. Service Battery numbered eighty men and I doubt that we dug more than twenty holes that night. The ground was frozen and digging was*

48. The 'Lucky Eleven' men of Service Battery, 924th Field Artillery Battalion who
escaped Büllingen by the skin of their teeth on 17 December 1944.
(Courtesy Stuart Bonne)

*pickaxe tough. The Captain's warning was legitimate as we could hear
small arms fire not far away. After an uneventful night, Captain Cobb
ordered us to 'Hurry up to the mess truck, have breakfast then pack up your
gear, bedrolls, barracks bags and weapons etc., we're moving back'. By the
time I returned from breakfast to my billet, German tanks were driving
down the street in front of our house. I stepped to the door to observe what
was happening and enemy machine-gun fire shattered the door in front of
me. Miraculously, it failed to hit me. Together, Chester Krawczyk, George
Matanich, Marvin Westbrook and I decided to try and escape. By this
time, German tanks and Halftrack personnel carriers were swarming all
over the place. There was an interval of about 75 yards between the German
vehicles as they motored down the street past our position. We decided to cross
the street using this gap in the column and joined some 2nd Division
engineers to fire on the enemy vehicles using rifles and carbines. We were
standing above the road and off the east side when one of the engineers
turned to me and said 'This isn't going to work, we had best try to get back
to the rear and report what is going on up here.' At this point, the four of us
headed for an old dilapidated barn across a nearby field, and then ran
towards a grove of trees in the distance. Our next objective was a
blacktopped road but the terrain proved to be a definite advantage to the
enemy as it sloped uphill to the rear. We began receiving small arms fire
seemingly from one person but one by one we made it over the hill and out
of sight. All this time I was peppering carbine rounds into a ravine from
where it appeared the German was firing at us. I kept him under fire to aid
our escape and upon reaching the highway from St. Vith, hailed a G.I.
gasoline truck full of empty five gallon gas cans.*

Boone and his group of three eventually made it to safety and lived to fight

Büllingen

(1) SV Btry/924 F.A. Bn. Btry command post.
(2) SV Btry/924 F.A. Bn. Truck park and supplies area.
(3) Sgt. Yager, Pvts Romaker and Madanado run to intercept Kampfgruppe Peiper with bazooka.
(4) Pfc. Goldstein and Cpl. Foehringer fire bazooka at tank.
(5) Kampfgruppe Peiper's route from Honsfeld through town.
(6) Route of KG-P unsuccessful probe to Krinkelt/Wirtzfeld.
(7) Escape route north to Elsenborn for SV/371 and 535 AAA AW.

(8) SV Btry/371 F.A. Bn. Truck park and supplies area.
(9) 2nd Division Artillery air strip.
(10) To 99th Division Artillery air strip.
(11) 535 AAA AW Btry command post area.
(12) To Butgenbach and 99th Division HQs.
(13) To Hunningen, Murringen and Losheim.
(14) Hotel Dahmen used by 12th VGD as aid station, post office across street facing hotel.

9. Sergeant James. W. Decker of the 535th Anti-Aircraft Automatic Weapons Battalion escaped from Büllingen as Kampfgruppe Peiper entered town on the Honsfeld road. (Courtesy James W. Decker)

another day. All told, eleven of Captain Cobb's men made it out of Büllingen that morning and earned themselves the nickname 'The Lucky Eleven'. On the southern outskirts of Büllingen, the Germans came upon two airstrips of the 2nd and 99th Divisional Artillery. The 2nd Division pilots and ground staff couldn't reach their planes in order to fly them out, so they called down their own artillery upon the airstrip to prevent the enemy capturing the planes intact. Ten of the eleven pilots on the 99th airstrip managed to fly their planes out right under the noses of approaching enemy tanks, earning themselves Distinguished Flying Crosses in the process. The eleventh plane had to be abandoned as it was undergoing maintenance at the time of the German attack. On the main street of Büllingen that morning, Sergeant James W. Decker of the 535th Anti-Aircraft Automatic Weapons Battalion was moving five of the unit's trucks into the village, when Peiper's tanks suddenly burst onto the main street from the Honsfeld direction. The leading tank stopped, backed up a few yards to get a better field of fire, and then opened up on Sergeant Decker and his men with its machine gun. Decker jumped out of his truck and raced for cover inside an adjacent building. From a window, he spotted six tanks, followed by twelve halftracks laden with *SS Panzergrenadiers*, racing though the village. As they did so, the

50. Main street, Büllingen looking west after the battle. (Courtesy Robert A. Green)

Germans fired at anything that moved. Decker and his men were Headquarters Battery troops and, as such, only carried small arms. Each of their trucks carried a mounted 50-caliber machine gun, which would have proven useless against armored vehicles. It was clear to Sergeant Decker that the enemy was moving rapidly through the village on their way to an objective elsewhere. Upon entering Büllingen, the *1st SS Panzer Regiment* had effectively cut the main supply route for both the 2nd and 99th US Infantry Divisions. Three tanks and several halftracks full of infantry from *SS Untersturmführer* Werner Sternebeck's spearhead element turned right on the main street then swung left past the church and north in the direction of Wirtzfeld, while the rest of the column turned left towards Möderscheid.

At his command post in the school at Wirtzfeld, Brigadier General John H. Hinds, commanding 2nd Infantry Division Artillery, had a perfect view of the road to Büllingen. Colonel Matt F.C. Konop commanding 2nd Infantry Division Special Troops had received an urgent telephone call from General

51. Lieutenant Colonel Matt F. C. Konop commander 2nd Division Special Troops at Wirtzfeld. (Courtesy Matt F. C. Konop)

52. Lieutenant Owen R. McDermott of 1st Platoon Company C, 644th Tank Destroyer Battalion, stands behind one of his M-10 Tank Destroyers positioned outside the bakery in Wirtzfeld on 17 December 1944. (Courtesy Owen R. McDermott)

Robertson, his division commander, at 06:30.

> *Konop, I want you to alert all units at once and organize a 'last ditch defense' of this command post. Enemy tanks have broken through on our right flank and are reported nearing Büllingen now. We also have reports of some enemy paratroopers landing northwest of us. I want you to get every man.*
>
> *Yes Sir, General, you recall that our defense platoon is out on special duty and all we have are three truck drivers and three hospital returnees.*
>
> *Yes, I know, but get any man you can lay your hands on and put them on the line.*
>
> *'Very well, sir!*

With the utmost urgency, General Hinds and Colonel Konop organized a defense line dominating the approaches from Büllingen. A heterogeneous force of bazooka teams, anti-aircraft halftracks armed with quadruple 50 caliber machine guns, riflemen, headquarters personnel and military police, took up positions on the southeastern edge of the village. Soon afterwards, a platoon of self-propelled tank destroyers of Company C, 644th Tank Destroyer Battalion, appeared on the scene. Lieutenant Owen R. McDermott, the platoon commander, placed his three guns on the Büllingerberg hill southeast of Wirtzfeld and overlooking the road

53. Lieutenant Owen R. McDermott of 1st Platoon, Company C, 644th Tank Destroyer Battalion at Wirtzfeld. (Courtesy Owen R. McDermott)

from Büllingen. Simultaneously, Lieutenant Carlo Biggio, Executive Officer of Battery C, 372nd Field Artillery Battalion, found himself on the north edge of Wirtzfeld receiving a phone call from his battalion commander Lieutenant Colonel Frank W. Mostek who, ordered him to rush a 155-mm howitzer to help defend his command post on the southern end of the village.

Shortly after General Hinds and Colonel Konop completed their defensive arrangements, Colonel Ralph W. Zwicker, the 2nd Infantry Division Chief of Staff called General Hinds and told him to displace his command post at once. Convinced his staff could stop any attack by the approaching German column, General Hinds outlined his defense plan to Colonel Zwicker. In view of his well-founded optimism, Colonel Zwicker granted him permission to remain in place.

As Lieutenant McDermott's men scanned the road to Büllingen, they heard the sound of armored vehicles approaching on the road below them and off to their right rear.

The German tanks and halftracks had circumvented the Büllingerberg, possibly trying to establish contact with the *12th SS Panzer Division* that by then should have taken Krinkelt. This manoeuver effectively had them moving west and around the northern tip of the hill towards Wirtzfeld. Moments later, a tank rumbled into view but, wishing to make a positive identification of the vehicle, McDermott's men held their fire. In recalling this action, many years later, Lieutenant McDermott said:

> *This hesitation worked out fine, as when I gave the order to fire, we had three tanks and an armored personnel carrier lined up like a shooting gallery.*

Standing near the church, Colonel Konop could clearly see the approaching enemy armor, followed by *SS Panzergrenadiers* on foot. Suddenly, machine-gun fire shattered the early morning air as bullets tore through the treetops behind Colonel Konop. Lieutenant McDermott's men opened fire, instantly hitting one of the tanks and setting it ablaze. A raging firefight broke out as German artillery fired a few rounds, which exploded in the vicinity of the small church. The defenders yielded not one inch and destroyed the German vehicles one at a time. Lieutenant Biggio well remembers that encounter with this group of enemy vehicles:

> *I march ordered my fastest crew and we dashed down the main street of Wirtzfeld to do battle with the tanks. On the south edge of town we quickly unlimbered and fired a round at the nearest tank (about 600 yards across an open field and clearly visible.) The round was over, and then two things happened: first, the gunner announced that he thought the tanks had already been knocked out, and second, a messenger arrived from battalion with a written message that we were not to fire except in an emergency because ammo re-supply was in doubt. Further observation verified that the German tanks were not firing. I later learned that the 644th Tank Destroyer Battalion had knocked them out moments before we arrived.*

All the while, General Hinds remained at his post, despite being under heavy small-arms and artillery fire that killed several of the men around him. For his part in this action, he earned the Bronze Star, the citation for which said:

> *Throughout the action General Hinds displayed great coolness and personal courage. Through his actions and example, he helped materially to prevent the enemy from overrunning the division headquarters position.*

Meanwhile, back in Büllingen, Sergeant James Decker discovered he had company in the form of three other men from his battery. They checked the building in which they had taken refuge and found another man from their unit, who was suffering from shell shock and bleeding from the ears. Sergeant Decker decided that their best move would be to leave Büllingen before the Germans discovered them. Time after time, as they tried to exit the building, they came under fire from enemy field guns located somewhere off to the southeast.

Throughout Büllingen, groups of American soldiers sought refuge wherever they could and determined to escape one way or another. Sergeant Grant Yager and his friends, taken prisoner on the Honsfeld road, rode into the village aboard the enemy halftrack and dismounted in the center. There, the Germans put them in the rear of a captured American truck along with other prisoners. The driver, a young wounded German, was unable to control the strange truck due to a wounded foot. He ran off the road into the ditch while still in town. Climbing out of the vehicle, he rounded up his prisoners and marched them to a large barn.

By mid morning, the fog had lifted and the sun appeared over the village. Along the Honsfeld road, Corporal Deloise Rapp lay motionless at the roadside. He heard the sound of planes circling over the area and raised his head to see what was happening. The planes were from the 389th and 390th US Fighter squadrons. One of them suddenly swooped down, strafing the road, which was packed with German vehicles. Tankers slammed shut their hatches and sought shelter as the plane passed repeatedly over the enemy column. Corporal Rapp seized the opportunity to crawl out of the ditch into a nearby field. On the far side of the hedge, to his surprise, he met Lieutenant Jack Varner. As the American pilot began another strafing run, the two men broke cover and ran across the field to a house about 150 yards distant. They ran into the basement to find three others sheltering inside. Two were GI engineers and the third, a Belgian civilian about fifty years of age. The civilian wanted to go home, but the Americans were frightened to let him go, so all five settled down in the cellar. By then, Corporal Rapp was in tremendous pain and unable to walk due to a bad leg wound. All five men were suffering from the intense cold.

To the northwest of Büllingen, on the high ground at a road

54. American engineers clean up in front of the church in Büllingen. (US Army photograph)

junction named Dom Bütgenbach, shortly after the passage of a few of Peiper's vehicles, two companies of the 254th Engineer Combat Battalion looked east in surprise as the bulk of the enemy column swung off to the south-west in the direction of Möderscheid. It seemed to the watching Americans that the enemy had missed a golden opportunity since in taking the road to Bütgenbach, Peiper could have reached Elsenborn and trapped both the 2nd and 99th Divisions. American observers attributed this change of direction to the appearance of US fighter-bombers. In reality, this raid had little effect upon the *Kampfgruppe Peiper* whose commander simply cut back to his prescribed route so as to leave Rollbahn 'C' to his running mate, the *12th SS Panzer Division*.

As the Germans passed through Büllingen, they subjected Sergeant Decker and his men of the 535th AA Weapons Battalion to intense mortar fire. Realizing their position was untenable, Decker and his buddies moved out onto the main street. Decker called out, identifying himself in the hope that other Americans in hiding would emerge to join them, but none appeared. Moving out of the village, they went west on the main road and upon reaching Dom Bütgenbach, established contact with friendly troops. Sergeant Decker informed a lieutenant of the situation in Büllingen and this officer advised him to head for Bütgenbach in the hope of re-joining his battalion. Weary, but safe, the anti-aircraft gunners set out on foot knowing that they had lived to fight another day.

Chapter Six

Losheimergraben – Mürringen

17 December 1944

By daylight on 17 December, the Germans were even more determined to capture the Losheimergraben crossroads and thus enable the *12th SS Panzer Division* to advance west along Rollbahn 'C'.

Oberstleutnant Wilhelm Osterhold, the youngest regimental commander in the *Wehrmacht* and a veteran of the bloody battles on the Russian front, was ready to resume his attack against the customs buildings and houses clustered around the crossroads. His opponents, the 1st Battalion, 394th Infantry had now pulled back to the west and occupied positions north of Buchholz station. Lieutenant Colonel John M. Hightower's 1st Battalion, 23rd Infantry held the, by then exposed, flank position in Hünningen. To their right rear, Peiper's column streamed along the Honsfeld to Büllingen road and it was now obvious to them that their position was dangerously

55. *The Losheimergraben crossroad in 1947.* (Hatlem Collection)

To Losheim

Chateau
Buffalo Bill

Co B Sgts Hilliard & Trent
and their platoons

Co D /394 Mortar Platoon
Command Post

48th Volksgrenadier
Regiment

56. *Lieutenant Colonel John M. Hightower (seated), commander of 1st Battalion 23rd Infantry pictured here in Normandy. In the Ardennes this unit defended Hünningen. (Courtesy William D. Amorello)*

exposed and that they risked total envelopment.

At 06:40, after a short artillery concentration, the Germans resumed their assaults against the 1st and 3rd Battalions 394th Infantry. *Oberstleutnant* Heinz Georg Lemm's *27th Fusilier Regiment* of the *12th Volksgrenadier Division* moved to flank Losheimergraben on the west as Osterhold's *48th Grenadier Regiment* continued its frontal attack. Lemm's fusiliers managed to penetrate the US line between the 1st and 3rd Battalions and by 11:00, were able to bring Rollbahn 'C' under small-arms fire.

Helmut Stiegler and other engineers found themselves attached to Osterhold's *48th Grenadier Regiment* on a minesweeping detail. They marched west up the railroad cutting and soon reached the infantry assembly area in the forest to the north of the railroad. Here they joined a group of about fifty infantrymen led by a scar-faced non-commissioned officer. Stiegler recognized the men as veterans, all in high spirits and armed with MP-40 machine pistols. They set off through the forest, led by the scar-faced sergeant in the direction of the 1st Battalion, 394th Infantry foxhole line west of the Lanzerath-Losheimergraben road. Suddenly, the sergeant waved his hand and his men dropped to the ground. 'Scarface' had spotted a US machine-gun position across the road. The Americans, seemingly unaware of what was happening, waved him forward. Calmly, he walked towards them, and then suddenly opened fire, urging his men to charge. A familiar cry of 'Hurrah!' went up as the *Grenadiers* rushed the American position. The machine gunners abandoned their weapon and fled to the west. *Generalmajor* Engel's men were a little nearer their goal; the capture of Losheimergraben.

Some 200 yards southeast of the vital crossroads, fifty men of Companies A and B, 394th Infantry, plus a few truck drivers, under the command of Lieutenant Dewey Plankers, were holding off German patrols. After several hours of backbreaking work, German engineers managed to erect a bridge across the railway northwest of Losheim. Three German *Sturmgeschutz* assault guns crossed the bridge with a rifle company and attacked Plankers' position through the forest. The Americans were by then low on ammunition, and withdrew towards the crossroads.

By early afternoon, it was obvious that the crossroads defenders couldn't hold out much longer. General Lauer ordered Colonel Douglas to commence a withdrawal with effect from 15:30. Once withdrawn, the 1st and 3rd Battalions were to fall back to positions on the high ground just west of Mürringen. The withdrawal from Losheimergraben could now begin.

At Losheimergraben, heavily armed German infantrymen were approximately 100 yards from the customs post. Colonel Douglas ordered his men to burn all maps and set off thermite grenades in his command post so as to deny its use to the enemy. Hearing an explosion at close quarters, he left the command post to discover that his jeep had received a direct hit. Fortunately, the only casualty other than the vehicle was the Colonel's musette bag containing his toothbrush, razor etc. Colonel Douglas and his command group set off on foot towards Mürringen.

The scar-faced German sergeant and his men now attacked a bivouac area of the 394th Regimental Anti-tank Company, destroying a jeep in the process. Searching the tents, the German infantrymen 'struck it rich'. They found a hoard of chocolate and cigarettes and stopped to take advantage of their find. As they did so, a German lieutenant arrived on the scene and, using a captured US radio, began sending out messages in English. After their short break, the German Grenadiers resumed their advance through the forest towards Mürringen.

Some 600 yards north of Losheimergraben Captain Simmons, of Company K, 394th Infantry, hadn't yet received orders to withdraw. Company K had received no further instructions from battalion since the previous evening. During the night, the 1st Battalion, 394th Infantry changed its radio call signs but failed to inform Company K, therefore all attempts by Simmons to contact the 1st Battalion command post using the SCR 300 radio set met without success. Captain Simmons realized that friendly units on either side of his company were pulling back and, at 13:00, he and his men came under attack. For seven minutes, Company K kept the attacking enemy pinned down with automatic weapon fire and mortars, but ammunition started running low. Simmons withdrew his company about 300 yards where, once again, they set up a hasty defense. Among the rows of conifers, each man from Company K fired a final volley at the enemy as he came within sight. So as to enable a speedy withdrawal, and take out all his wounded men, Captain Simmons ordered his mortar crews to abandon their weapons. Their ammunition exhausted, the Company K GIs set out towards Krinkelt. By then, most of the 1st and 3rd Battalions were heading west except for isolated small units scattered throughout the area. Among these units was the Losheimergraben crossroads rearguard under Lieutenant Plankers, still holding onto the customs houses and other buildings clustered around the road junction. Towards late afternoon, realizing that he and his men were in a hopeless situation, Plankers ordered the survivors to try and escape in the direction of Mürringen. Many never made it out and ended up by being either killed or captured in the final German assault. Among those captured was Private William P. Kirkbride of the 1st Platoon, 394th Anti-tank Company who well remembers that second day at Losheimergraben:

> On the morning of 17 December, we heard new action all around us. Armor was moving south and behind us. The Company B commander walked through our area from the front. He told us the entire front was gone and that he was the only one to get out of his company command post. Our telephone was out and we needed new orders. Our staff sergeant came back and decided to go to our platoon leader's command post for orders and/or information. About noon, we hitched the antitank gun up to our 6x6 Dodge truck and drove north to Losheimergraben where we turned east and parked between two of the customs' houses. First Lieutenant Gifford Benson, our platoon leader and Tech Sergeant Piar were both gone. There were about fifteen other guys present from mixed outfits so with our squad, this made about twenty-five soldiers. We entered the basement of one of the houses to find a very young-looking fellow lying face down on the floor dressed in the uniform of a U.S. second lieutenant. Nobody knew who he was and some thought he was shell-shocked, as he wouldn't talk to anyone. I got down on the floor beside him and spoke very gently in his ear as he turned his head and looked at me, without saying a word. He was not shaking or crying; he just stared at me for a while; he seemed scared. I made sure he wasn't wounded then decided to leave him alone as he was in no condition to lead us. We set up a perimeter defense and waited, as no one seemed to know what to do next. At this time, a German assault gun (Sturmgeschutz) started moving up the main road towards us. Someone told me there were three tanks (actually assault guns), one of which was almost in sight just east of the customs' houses. We (incorrectly) believed it to be a Panther tank. Mel Weidner and I were at the northeast basement window and he suggested we get a bazooka and go for the assault gun. When the enemy vehicle cleared the corner and was in clear range, he fired one rocket, which hit it - dead center on its left side. After a few minutes, the driver tried to stand up then looked our way and fell back into the vehicle. The other two assault guns backed off.

Oberstleutnant Osterhold also witnessed the knocking out of this same *Sturmgeschutz*:

> A bazooka hit the left track immobilizing the vehicle. It couldn't use its gun, as you had to turn the whole vehicle in order to give the gun its maximum traversing capability. The defenders put a 57mm antitank gun at the corner of one of the customs houses (Kirkbride's squad) but it could

only hit the front of the 'Stug' and the shells just bounced off it. We were therefore obliged to capture the houses in order to rescue the driver and three crewmen.

By then, *48th Grenadier Regiment* began moving to capture the buildings, going as its commander recalls 'Straight through the easternmost house which was unoccupied and firing at the basement windows of the middle house.'

Inside the house, Bill Kirkbride could see Osterhold's men closing in on the buildings:

> *The Germans were slipping closer all around us. There were other houses south of us with some outbuildings to the east along a hedgerow we could see the German infantrymen moving closer and just before darkness, we decided to give up as we didn't know what else to do. We didn't want to go through the night with the enemy close enough to throw grenades through our basement windows. Once we'd decided to surrender, no one wanted to go out and face the Germans. We stuck a white flag out of the south window and I then saw a German officer whom I presume to have been Osterhold. When we displayed our flag, he immediately came forward to the house, asking if we wanted to surrender. When I saw him leave cover and approach our flag, I immediately surmised that he trusted us not to shoot him, therefore I also believed that he wouldn't shoot us so I volunteered to go out and talk to him. He was of average size, very cleanly dressed, clean shaven and spoke good English.*

Oberstleutnant Osterhold informed Kirkbride that if he and his buddies didn't surrender Osterhold's men had the capability to destroy the customs' house. Kirkbride returned to the basement where he and his fellow Americans started to strip down their weapons. Osterhold then came into the basement and told the anxious GIs to hurry up. The Americans emerged to be taken prisoner and the German commander told them to go to their vehicles and get their personal belongings. He well remembers this incident:

> *I warned them to be cautious, 'Hide it when you can! Your watch etc. because later on there might be people who are 'courageous' enough to take it away from you. With combat prisoners, we had some feeling of solidarity, even with the Russians. We fighting outfits were the same poor dogs doing the dirty work!*

Osterhold advised his prisoners to pick up whatever rations they could, as it would take a few days to get them to a prison camp. Later that evening, about 150 men of *Oberstleutnant* Otto Skorzeny's *150th Panzer Brigade* passed through Losheimergraben, some wearing American uniforms and driving captured American vehicles. Much to his annoyance, Osterhold learned that Skorzeny's men had relieved the prisoners of some items of clothing. Upon hearing of this, he later sent a captured truckload of US clothing back through the lines to catch up with the prisoners. He never found out whether it ever reached them or not.

As the Germans captured Losheimergraben, Lieutenant Jack Varner and Corporal Deloise Rapp were still hiding in a Büllingen cellar. Rapp couldn't move since his right leg and foot were severely swollen. At about 16:00, the Belgian civilian pleaded to be allowed to leave and promised he wouldn't disclose their whereabouts to the Germans, so against their better judgment, they let him go. Half an hour later, they heard the ominous clank of German tank tracks outside the basement door and the whine of a moving turret told them the worst. Outside, in the bitter cold of dusk, a heavily accented voice called out in broken English 'Come out, come out, we have a surprise for you!' Lieutenant Varner started up the cellar steps, his hands raised above his head. The two engineers picked up Corporal Rapp and carried him outside into the cold evening air. As the emerged onto the dingy street, the German tank cannon pointed menacingly at the cellar door.

North of Losheimergraben, the Germans attacked the 2nd Battalion, 394th Infantry with renewed vigor on 17 December, from the direction of Udenbreth. Captain Robert R. McGee Jr. the battalion operations officer, told his memories of this day in a combat interview at a house in Elsenborn about a month later:

> On the morning of 17 December, we kept looking for the 1st Battalion, 393rd Infantry, on our left flank and kept getting reports from Regiment that they were trying to push a force forward to make contact with that unit. We didn't know it then, but during the night, the Germans had worked in throughout the 1st Battalion, 393rd area and had seriously chewed it up. During the morning, light and sporadic artillery hit us until about 11:00, although there seemed to be terrific firefights going on to either side of us. I later learned that the 1st and 3rd Battalions of our regiment had also been heavily engaged. About 11:00, a German patrol hit our right flank, but Company G routed them when they threw in mortar fire then opened up with small arms.
>
> All hell seemed to be breaking loose on our flanks and the situation worsened when Captain Boyd M. McCune, the assistant regimental operations officer arrived at the battalion command post at about 14:15 with orders to withdraw to a tentative line on a map overlay. The order called for retrograde movement to commence at 15:00 and we informed the companies of the withdrawal plan. The move back was to be to the vicinity of Weisserstein and Captain McCune told us that a battalion of the 2nd Infantry Division had gone into position around Honsfeld (actually Hünningen) and that conditions looked bad.
>
> The shortness of time between receipt of the order and the execution of its mission was a serious problem, although this didn't give the battalion staff too much cause for worry since the withdrawal route led over ground with which the company commanders were familiar. The withdrawal did not begin on time however.

Captain Ben W. Legare, the 2nd Battalion Executive Officer moved out first in command of the battalion transport. He arrived in Mürringen around 19:00 and upon reaching the regimental command post, informed Colonel Don Riley, the regimental commander of the state of the battalion. According to Legare, during the incoming enemy artillery barrage on the first day, the 2nd Battalion Commander had 'Gone to pieces'. He had taken refuge in his command post and cowered in a corner throughout the first day. During the entire action, he offered not one word of assistance and his entire staff almost forgot his presence, except when someone inadvertently stumbled over him. Under cover of darkness, he left the command post to relieve himself under supervision. Captain McGee assigned two enlisted men to assist the commander, by then reduced to a quivering hulk, during the withdrawal. Major Legare informed Colonel Riley that the bulk of the 2nd Battalion infantry led by Captain McGee was still in the forest to the east between Mürringen and the International Highway. Legare and his men then took up defensive positions around the regimental command post. Staff Sergeant Rex W. Whitehead, of Company H, 394th, recalls that move back toward Mürringen:

> *The phone rang, and someone told Failor that we were going to withdraw in fifteen minutes and that we were to get all our guns and ammo on the road. We carried on for about fifteen minutes when Barney came up in his jeep and said to throw on the mortars and forget the ammo. He said that he would be back after us. We went back to the hut to get our stuff together and the phone rang. They told us that the road was cut (Rollbahn B), so for us to wait on the road and go with Company G, when they came along. We threw all we could carry in our sleeping bags and left what we thought we wouldn't need. Just as we were leaving, one of the guys said that I had a package there. I couldn't carry it, so, I tore it open to find several little packages, nicely wrapped Christmas gifts. I opened the larger one and it was a cake, so I gave each guy a piece of it and then pushed the other things in my bag. We gave out all the ammo, but most of us had pistols and knew that you didn't need much, for they weren't any good anyway. I put about ten 'D-Bars' in my pockets, and we went over to the road. Elements of the 3rd Battalion went by us and we waited for about ten minutes, but didn't see anyone from Company G. We knew that there was no one behind us, and decided to take off. We started walking up California Road (the International Highway) toward the 'Corduroy Road' (Rollbahn B) the 2nd Battalion MSR. There was no one in sight, and we started to throw things away, for we had far too much to carry very far. I had burned all my stamped envelopes, for I had written my address on all of them. We could hear*

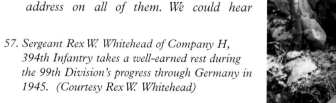

57. Sergeant Rex W. Whitehead of Company H, 394th Infantry takes a well-earned rest during the 99th Division's progress through Germany in 1945. (Courtesy Rex W. Whitehead)

vehicles to the rear and knew that there was very little chance that they were ours. We walked about a mile up the road when we saw two jeeps coming down the road toward us. When they came nearer, we could see that they were our squad jeeps and our drivers, Qualkenbush and Stewart along with Payne, the transportation corporal. They stopped and yelled for us to 'Get the Hell in!' so we piled on the trailers, which were filled with bedrolls and ammo, and they turned around and took off. I never want to take another ride like that one, as the road was icy and they had the jeeps wide open. We later found out that Donkers had given us up, when Carpenter said that they couldn't do that and asked for a couple of jeeps and two men who would try to get through to us even if the roads were out. Our drivers and Payne said that they would go, and they probably saved us by doing that. We turned onto the 'Corduroy Road' and there was a 2^1/$_2$-ton truck there in the mud. I remember wondering if the driver had perhaps booby-trapped it and, as an afterthought, thought that I should at least shoot out the tires.

We would jump off the jeep whenever we approached a hole in the log road and push the jeep through if it was stopped. We passed a Jerry gas tank that had been dropped (by parachute) that morning and through the old platoon area. We'd gone about two miles and still hadn't seen any of our troops. As we rounded the corner by the battalion command post, Captain Legare was there and told us to pour it on and catch up to the convoy. Some of the boys said they saw Fred Zimmerman's body lying there at the side of the road. (Sergeant Frederick F. Zimmerman's remains would be recovered in late May of 2001).

We went around another corner, and there were the boys from the other sections, to the side of the road carrying their mortars and ammo. They sort of cheered when they saw us, for we had been given up as lost. We would have been if Donkers the 'Groundhog' had had his way. We went past the men and soon found the rear of the regimental convoy. As we slowed down, we looked back to see that shells were landing on the area where we'd just seen the rest of our boys. I was feeling damn sorry for them when the barrage lifted and we caught some of the shells, and at that time, I shifted the sorrow to myself. We jumped off the vehicle and got in an old ack-ack emplacement, then shortly afterwards the convoy moved on again. We came to the top of a hill and Judge was mumbling something about 'On maneuvers, they would get busted for stopping on a hill, and look at this.' A jeep came by with someone on it that had been hit. On the left side of the road, looking down into a long wide draw, tracers were going back and forth between the two hills. - They were firing at each other, but why didn't they fire at the vehicles? We were lined up like clay pigeons - it beats me, unless they were both our men firing at each other, which would not have been hard to figure out in that situation. We all felt that the 99th was the disgrace of the army, for we were shagging out without a fight. I found out later that that wasn't true.

We moved on and came to a little town (Mürringen) and just as we pulled into the middle of it, by a crossroads, Payne came back and said, 'Get out and start digging in'. Just then, a shell came in - big stuff, for you could hear it coming, and we needed no more advice. I jumped over a fence into a little lot and had started digging when Judge yelled 'Whitey, come over here, we have a hole'. He had found a slit trench and he and Merle were in it. I leapt in just as a couple of shells came in hitting the crossroads. Just then Qually came tearing over and told us to move over for he was coming in. Judge and I were on the bottom with the others on top. The Krauts were zeroing in on that road. It was my first real 'sweat job' and for some reason, I wasn't scared. Maybe I was so frightened that I didn't realize it, but I don't think I was. Funny, but the first thing I could think of was an article I had read in the 'Infantry Journal' on 'How to combat fear' and remembered them saying, to crack a joke and relieve the tension. Well, I had been eating a D-Bar, and so I said to Judge, 'How about a bite of D-Bar, Judge?' Just then, one landed so close that it shook us in the hole, 'F—— the D-Bar,' said Judge, and he meant it, but I believe it helped for a minute. Qually was very frightened for he kept muttering something that might have been a prayer. Probably was, for I did a little of it myself.

The shelling let up and someone yelled to come over there, for they had a house with a good cellar in it. We ran, but 'Schnell' to the building across the street and filed into the cellar. It was filled with water but had boards to sit on and a rock roof, which made us feel safer, but I doubt if it was. Several drivers I didn't know came down and we stayed there while a few more shells hit the town. They said that the name of the place was Mürringen, and that it was where our kitchens had been. The day before, the Company F kitchen had a shell land fifteen yards from it without a single casualty. There were some bottles that looked like Cognac, but no one seemed to want any of it.

Failor said he was going to contact officers and see what was going on and moved out. In a while, he came back and said for us to come out and that we were going to contact 3rd Battalion and stay with them. We walked back up the road we had come in on, about a hundred men, I guess, with Captain Legare and Major Kriz leading. We stood around for a while, as the officers debated what to do, for they couldn't contact the 3rd Battalion, so we went back into town. I stayed in a house with Lieutenant Reed to act as a runner, and the rest of them went back to the same house we were in earlier. I tried to get a little sleep on the stairs of the house, and then an officer wanted to know where our section was, so I took him to the house to see Failor. I found Judge, Guy and Beaver in an upstairs room. They'd found a lot of K Rations and were really tearing into them, as this was the first food they'd had in three days, apart from D-Bars. I ate a few, and then threw some down the cellar to the guys, and then Merle said, 'Follow me.' We went into another room and there was a bed so we lay down. Even if the situation didn't call for comfort, it was the first bed I'd been on since we left England, so it was pretty nice.

Failor came back and said that we were going to 'Get the Hell out of here'. He asked Merle, 'Think you can drive a jeep?' Merle answered 'Hell, Yes!' They moved out and were back in a few minutes so we all crawled onto the two jeeps they had. They told us they had stolen them and that we were getting out of there. The officers didn't know what the hell we were going to do and were lost. Fleck got cold and started to unroll a bedroll that was on the trailer. He started to laugh and said, 'so you stole some jeeps, huh? Well you stole our own damn vehicles!' We laughed at that. In the distance, parachute flares were dropping and tracer fire climbed high in the sky. A few flares went up around us and we all froze, I felt damned conspicuous. After a while, Failor came back and said that he couldn't find the guy he was supposed to meet, so we went back to the house. When we got there, a runner came up and told us that we were moving out. We all filled our canteens then got on the three quarter ton maintenance truck with Meyers driving and the Chaplain in front, but I didn't know it then. His jeep had been lost. We moved out of town away from the front, but the front was everywhere then. There were burp gunners all over town and we got out just in time. I rode on the tailgate wrapped up in a blanket for it was quite cold with snow on the ground.

About one third of each infantry platoon in the 2nd Battalion had remained in position as the vehicles pulled out for Mürringen and the battalion command post group moved a little further west to establish the new command post. Battalion headquarters then ordered the companies to come out using three trails and firebreaks. The command group then moved out along a minor trail called the 'Odepfad' where they eventually met up with men from Company C of the 1st Battalion. Captain McGee and the fifty men with him tied in with Company C for the night as their radio was growing very weak and it was proving difficult to maintain contact with the 2nd Battalion Rifle Companies. Eventually, however, they worked out a system whereby every hour or so, they could have Company E check in with them. Any instructions for the rest of the battalion would be given to Company E who would then relay them to the rest of the battalion. This contact began about 19:00 and was successfully retained throughout the night.

Staff Sergeant Harold F. Schaefer, of Company G, 394th Infantry wrote down his memories of the infantry withdrawal in an article he sent the author:

Shortly after 15:00 hours, the word came down to pack combat packs with rations and as much ammo as we had or could carry and get ready to move out. We all thought that this was going to be a combat patrol, ignoring the fact that we didn't usually take rations. When the 2nd Platoon left their positions and assembled in the company command post area, and the rest of the company was there, we began to realize that this was something more than a combat patrol. At this time, we learned that the Krauts had broken through our lines to the north and south of us, and we were withdrawing to the battalion command post area. We blew a kiss back to the area we had left and said goodbye to the half-completed letter home, the remainder of the box of cookies we were self-rationing...and the other personal gear that we would probably never see again.

We moved out, heading west on a fire trail and met some of our Company H machine gunners. They asked us where the hell we were going. They hadn't gotten the word, but gathered their equipment and tagged onto our column. The smooth bores (Rex Whitehead and his buddies) had left earlier by vehicle and were now in Mürringen with regiment. Reaching the International Highway, we turned north. Looking south, we saw a platoon-sized unit coming up the highway. They were part of Company C, 394th Infantry who had been left in the woods when the rest of the company went south to support Company B. They had tried to go south but the Germans were blocking the highway and preventing them from re-joining their company, so they decided to move north. They joined our column and we headed north for the 2nd Battalion command post. We didn't go too great a distance before we turned into the forest on the west side of the road. We had now been pushed back

58. Sergeant Harold F. Schafer of 1st Squad, 2nd Platoon, Company G, 394th Infantry. (Courtesy Harold F. Schafer)

from our enviable position 'Somewhere in Germany' into Belgium without most of us firing a shot. We met Companies E and F in the new battalion command post area and set up a perimeter defense for the night. We thought we were defending battalion headquarters, but the commanding officer, staff (Captain McGee), and party had become lost and spent the night with Company C, 393rd Infantry. Company E had radio contact with battalion so we knew where they were. None of us would claim a good night's sleep that night, but we were in relatively good spirits. Ignorance is bliss.

The remnants of the 394th Infantry gathering around Mürringen were given a short breathing spell as the Germans concentrated on Lieutenant Colonel John M. Hightower's 1st Battalion, 23rd Infantry defending Hünningen some 1,500 yards further south. *Oberstleutnant* Osterhold's *48th Grenadier Regiment* badly mauled around Losheimergraben, re-formed on the high ground between the forest edge and Mürringen. The north flank of the 394th Infantry now lay exposed to the risk of counter-attack. *Oberst* Viebig's *277th Volksgrenadier Division* had been checked in its attempts to capture Krinkelt-Rocherath. *Generalmajor* Gerhard Engel of the *12th Volksgrenadier Division* ordered *Oberstleutnant* Heinz-Georg Lemm's *27th Fusilier Regiment* to capture Hünningen. Hightower and his men faced a difficult task in trying to defend the village. It faced south and east in the direction of any advance from Losheimergraben or Honsfeld. Peiper's penetration had opened up the Honsfeld to Büllingen road, thereby exposing Hünningen to attack from the rear. That morning, as dawn broke over the battlefield, the 1st Battalion, 23rd Infantry found themselves with Germans, in strength, to their east, south and west.

The morning of 17 December brought with it limited visibility. First Lieutenant William Amorello commanded the Ammunition and Pioneer Platoon of Headquarters Company, Hightower's 1st Battalion. In the early morning light of 17 December, Lieutenant Amorello looked through his binoculars as Peiper's armored column made its way from Honsfeld to Büllingen. Unfortunately, the 2nd Division Artillery could not hit the Honsfeld to Büllingen road but could provide interdictory fire on the fields to the battalion front. In an audio taped account he sent the author, Lieutenant Amorello told of his experiences in Hünningen on the second day of the German attack:

> As the fog began to lift, I could see vehicles, tanks about half a mile away, like a silhouette, coming into view and then disappearing and as they disappeared more came in. How the hell they got behind us I don't know. The artillery that was coming in from the Germans was the most horrific I had ever seen and was only comparable to the bombardment we gave the Germans on Hill 192 the morning we attacked to take St. Lo. Shells were dropping all around us, constantly as Colonel Hightower ordered me to set up a defense of the battalion command post. We had plenty of machine guns and bazookas and even took cases of TNT and set them up at the edge of the woods in case anyone tried to come through. During the morning, twelve Mark IV tanks appeared to the south of the village. They assembled at the edge of the woods, some eight hundred yards from the American foxhole line. It is possible that these tanks were trying to seek refuge from the U.S. fighter-bombers then strafing and bombing the Honsfeld to Büllingen road. A towed three-inch antitank gun of the 801st Tank Destroyer Battalion, which had escaped from Honsfeld, knocked out four of these tanks with its first six shots. The remaining eight tanks made a hasty withdrawal.

Shortly after noon on 17 December, about 120 men of the 2nd and 254th Engineer Combat Battalions reinforced Hightower's battalion, having become separated from their units. Colonel Hightower sent them to form a roadblock against a possible enemy attack from the direction of Büllingen. Throughout the afternoon, the whole 1st Battalion position was subjected to heavy concentrations of 170-mm and 240-mm German artillery. At 16:00, the enemy launched a concentrated attack against Hightower's men, preceded by six minutes of furious shelling. The Colonel, nicknamed 'Big John' by his men, was a cool, calm man and rushed forward some 500 yards to be with his forward elements. Enemy fire forced him to abandon his jeep, but undeterred, he ran and crawled the remaining 200 yards to one of his forward command posts. As the shelling stopped, *Oberstleutnant* Lemm's *27th Fusilier Regiment* advanced on Hünningen from the southeast. First Lieutenant Charles W. Stockell, a forward observer with the 37th Field Artillery Battalion, was with Company B facing the wood line. Stockell

raced back across the open fields to the imposing stone church where he climbed a series of fragile ladders inside the steeple. From this new vantage point, he brought down shellfire upon the attacking *Volksgrenadiers* and from their foxholes, the men of Captain Kay Cowan's Company B, racked the attackers with automatic fire killing about fifty of them in the process. The remainder withdrew. *Oberstleutnant* Lemm launched six further attacks during the afternoon and early evening but each attack ran into a hail of small-arms and mortar fire that stopped the enemy soldiers dead in their tracks. Lieutenant Stockell remained in the church most of the day with his radio operator, during which direct fire from German artillery or tanks hit the steeple at least ten times. This fire eventually forced the two courageous artillerymen down the steeple, step by step, at the end of which their observation post was severely damaged.

59. Lieutenant Charles W. Stockell a Forward Artillery Observer with the 37th Field Artillery Battalion supported the 1st Battalion 23rd Infantry from his observation post in the church steeple in Hünningen. (Courtesy Charles W. Stockell)

A seventh attack by the Germans succeeded in breaking through part of Company B's wide front. Colonel Hightower, who was nearby, contacted a platoon of Company A, in position just north of Hünningen. Taking personal command of this platoon, he placed it in the gap while under heavy small-arms fire from enemy troops some thirty yards distant. He directed his men in hand-to-hand fighting and his courageous leadership inspired them to repel the enemy yet once again. Lieutenant Stockell managed to adjust a V Corps Artillery Battalion on the enemy assembly area in the woods to the southeast and, in the words of Captain F. Luchowski, the 1st Battalion operations officer, 'gave them Hell!' Despite numerous attempts, the Germans failed to capture the village. Lieutenant Stockell later reported, 'I had never seen the bodies as thick, very few wounded survived. In the darkness, if a man got hit crossing a field in heavy snow, he disappeared from sight. He just lay where he fell and froze or bled to death. Weapons lay in heaps amid the confusion of twisted frozen remains.'

As the evening of 17 December wore on, Colonel Hightower contacted Colonel Don Riley of the 394th Infantry and asked permission to withdraw from positions that were fast becoming untenable. At about 22:00, he received a radio message relayed by Lieutenant Stockell's SCR 610 radio. This radio was by then, the only remaining link with American units outside of Hünningen since all wires were cut and all batteries 'dead'. The message informed Hightower that his battalion was no longer attached to the 99th Division. The 1st Battalion was now under the control of Colonel Chester J. Hirchfelder's 9th (Manchu) Infantry Regiment of the 2nd Infantry Division.

At 23:00, Colonel Hirschfelder reached Hightower over the radio and told him that Hünningen and Mürringen were almost surrounded and went on to say that if the 1st Battalion expected to withdraw, it must move at once. Colonel Hightower replied that since he was in close contact with the enemy, immediate withdrawal was not possible. His men were engaged in hand-to-hand combat and he had to consider that he was protecting the right flank of Colonel Riley's 394th Infantry. Hirschfelder agreed and told Hightower to use his own judgment. Shortly before midnight, a lieutenant of the 2nd Battalion, 23rd Infantry, arrived at Hightower's command post with an eight-man patrol. He came in to lead Colonel Hightower's men to positions pre-arranged by Colonel Hirschfelder. Just after midnight, the German attack lost its impetus enough to permit withdrawal by the 1st Battalion. Hightower called his company commanders together and made tentative plans for their withdrawal to commence at 02:00. As the company commanders returned to their units, their commanding officer contacted Colonel Riley to clarify the situation. Riley told him that he (Riley) had no instructions to withdraw. Colonel Hightower now found himself on the horns of an uncomfortable dilemma.

In Mürringen, the 394th Infantry had not been hard pressed, although they had received their fair share of enemy shellfire. They had very little ammunition left and, despite having held onto many of their heavy weapons, could only make a stand if re-supplied with ammunition. Initially, Colonel Riley had hoped this might be possible by air, but this was a vain hope in view of bad weather conditions. The only alternative was for the 394th to withdraw north to Krinkelt using the one road still open.

Chapter Seven

Krinkelterwald

17 December 1944

At 01:00 on 17 December, the Germans began a fresh bombardment of all known US troop locations. Colonel Allen's 3rd Battalion, 393rd Infantry, although virtually surrounded, prepared to counterattack and re-establish its original line. In order to do so, the 3rd Battalion would have to capture the eastern end of Rollbahn 'A'.

Colonel Allen's men began their attack at 08:00 and started moving uphill and east of their battalion command post area. Shortly before reaching the summit of the east bank of the Jansbach Creek they ran into a fresh battalion of enemy infantry and a fierce firefight broke out. *Oberst* Viebig was determined to catch up on lost time and had called upon the *12th SS Panzer Division (Hitlerjugend)* to support his men. At about 09:30 *Brigadeführer* Hugo Kraas, Commander of the '*Hitlerjugend*', responded by committing the 2nd Battalion, *25th SS Panzergrenadier Regiment* under the command of *Obersturmbannführer* Richard Schulze-Kossens supported by several tank destroyers (*Jagdpanzers*). This initial force made up the lead element of *Kampfgruppe* Müller, commanded by SS *Obersturmbannführer* Siegfried

60. *Brigadeführer Hugo Kraas, commander of 12th SS Panzer Division 'Hitlerjugend'. (Taylor Library)*

Müller. The deployment of *Kampfgruppe* Müller constituted an important change of plan for the '*Hitlerjugend*'. Events on 16 December caused the *6th Panzer Army* planners to make this change within hours of the start of the attack. The joint attacks by the *12th* and *277th Volksgrenadier Divisions* had come up against far more determined resistance by the 99th Division than was foreseen by the German planners. By this, the second day

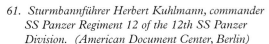

61. *Sturmbannführer Herbert Kuhlmann, commander SS Panzer Regiment 12 of the 12th SS Panzer Division. (American Document Center, Berlin)*

of the attack the Germans made the capture of Rollbahns 'A', 'B' and 'C' a top priority.

The lead German vehicle, a 20-mm flak gun, entered the forest at the bend in the International Highway then drove downhill on Rollbahn 'A' crossing the Olef and proceeding to the crest of the west bank of the creek. It stopped on the Wingertsknipp Hill just short of Colonel Allen's command post as a firefight broke out between the 3rd Battalion and the *SS Panzergrenadier*s. Four American bazooka teams moved forward, using the roadside ditches as cover and one of them succeeded in immobilizing the lead *Jagdpanzer*. Heavy small-arms fire raged back and forth in the midst of which the Battalion Chaplain Carl M. Truesdale and his assistant, Tech 5 Lloyd K. Herren, dodged shell bursts and bullets to distribute candy bars to the battling GIs. The enemy pressure increased with four more German vehicles inching forward and the 3rd Battalion attempt to regain its positions floundered. As American casualties mounted and ammunition began to run out, Colonel Allen informed the regiment in Krinkelt that his situation was fast becoming desperate.

62. *Obersturmbannführer Richard Schulze-Kossen, former aide to Adolf Hitler who served as a battalion commander in SS Panzergrenadier Regiment 25. (Courtesy Richard Schulze-Kossens)*

63. *Chaplain Carl M. Truesdale the Chaplain for 3rd Battalion, 393rd Infantry. (Courtesy Lloyd Herren)*

Sergeant Vernon L. McGarity of Company L grabbed a rocket launcher and braved heavy enemy fire to reach a better firing position. He wasted no time in shouldering his weapon to knock out the leading tank. His squad drove off the accompanying *SS Panzergrenadiers* with heavy small-arms fire and the remaining three tanks pulled back. At great personal risk, McGarity then rescued a wounded GI and went on to direct fire against a light gun, which the Germans had brought up to clear resistance from the area. Under fire, the intrepid sergeant ran to an ammunition hole to get what ammunition he could. By then, the attacking SS men had placed a machine gun to the rear of his squad, cutting off its only escape route. In a mad rage, McGarity leapt from his hole

64. *Sergeant Vernon L. McGarity of Company L, 393rd Infantry earned himself his nation's highest award, the Medal of Honor on the east bank of the Jansbech Creek before being captured by the attacking Germans. (US Army photograph)*

65. *Charles B. Macdonald and Will Cavanagh revisit the battlefield in 1988. (Author's collection)*

and killed the German machine gunners with his rifle. He then prevented all attempts to re-man this weapon. Finally, he and his squad ran out of ammunition and the Germans closed in taking them prisoner.

To the west on the far side of the Jansbach creek, Captain Charles B. MacDonald's Company I, 23rd Infantry, could hear Colonel Allen's men fighting for their very lives. As shells passed overhead, MacDonald listened attentively to First Lieutenant Gordon Jackman of Battery B, 370th Field Artillery Battalion as he used his artillery observer's radio to communicate with the 105-mm howitzers to the rear. Lieutenant Jackman commanded a four-man observation team comprising himself, Sergeant Norman J. Zewe, Tech 5 Arthur J. Hoffman and Tech 5 Guy W. Duren. This team had joined the 3rd Battalion, 23rd Infantry on its fire support observation mission the previous day. Guy Duren wrote of his experiences on the west bank of the Jansbach a few months later while on occupation duty in Germany:

66. *Private First Class Richard E. Cowan, a machine gunner with 3rd Battalion 23rd Infantry, earned himself the Medal of Honor in the battle to hold the West Bank of the Jansbach Creek. (Courtesy Bob Cowan)*

> *For breakfast the next morning, 17 December, we had toast from the stove with marmalade and coffee. It was fine. Just as I finished, Zewe found me. He said I must move the jeep back with the vehicles of the 23rd Infantry Regiment and that Company I had lost a quarter of their men in the shelling so things were not looking so hot. As I drove the jeep back to the rear about 400 yards on the 'road', I saw Perrine fixing a flat on a weapons carrier at the roadside. I drove into the woods on the left side of the road and straddling a large log until I hung up. I walked back and helped Perrine change his tire then he pulled my jeep off the log. Perrine had come forward that morning with Smith the wire corporal, Captain Fuetsch and Morgan. Captain Fuetsch was to act as liaison officer for the 3rd Battalion, 23rd Infantry. Smith and Perrine had laid wire back to the Fire Direction Center and set up a switchboard in the woods with Morgan as switchboard operator.*

An urgent message over Lieutenant Jackman's radio gave the beleaguered soldiers of 3rd Battalion, 393rd Infantry permission to pull out and they confirmed their intention to do so but

67. *Major General Walter M. Robertson presents an award to Hugh Burger of Company I, 23rd Infantry. (US Army photograph)*

stated that they'd have to leave their aid station behind to care for the seriously wounded. Colonel Jean D. Scott, commanding the 393rd Infantry, ordered his 1st and 3rd Battalions to take up new positions about one and a half miles east of Rocherath. Captain MacDonald called his platoon leaders on the radio and warned them to be on the lookout for the withdrawing men of the 393rd Infantry. He made it clear that the Germans would probably follow hot on the heels of the withdrawing Americans. He then took stock of his unit's predicament. There they were, a single rifle battalion, thinly dispersed in a densely forested area with orders to 'Hold on at all cost'. There were no reserves available and their only anti-tank defense consisted of Lieutenant Miller's Sherman tanks and in the case of Company I, one damaged bazooka with three rockets.

69. Sergeant Raymond L. Savage, the Communications Sergeant for Company I, 23rd Infantry. (Courtesy Hugh Burger)

To the east, Colonel Allen's 3rd Battalion, 393rd Infantry, prepared to withdraw. Medics loaded wounded men onto every available vehicle. Captain Frederick J. MacIntyre, the battalion surgeon, volunteered to stay behind with a few of his men and the more seriously wounded. Before they left the command post area, Colonel Allen ordered his men to destroy radios, telephone switchboards and all non-portable equipment. At around noon, the 3rd Battalion began its move to the west. Vehicles carrying the wounded moved out first, followed by the rifle companies with Captain Roland L. Neudecker's Company L acting as the rearguard. The Germans put pressure on Company L which pulled back in stages, fighting and disengaging by degrees. Running a gauntlet of machine-gun and mortar fire, Captain Neudecker's rearguard moved west and across the Jansbach.

Upon reaching Captain Macdonald's roadblock, the remnants of Colonel Allen's battalion paused briefly to donate their few remaining clips of ammunition and grenades to the GIs of Company I. Although MacDonald didn't know it, his battalion was all that stood in the way of the Germans cutting off all 2nd Division and 99th Division troops engaged in the attack north of Rocherath. General Robertson, the 2nd Division Commander, was well aware of the situation, hence his decision to fight a delaying action east of Krinkelt-Rocherath. This action would extend south of Wirtzfeld so as to protect his only possible withdrawal route, – the secondary road from Wirtzfeld to Elsenborn. The 2nd Engineer Battalion worked all out to make this road useable to one-way traffic.

Earlier that day, at about 10:00, General Robertson left his command post on the northern edge of Wirtzfeld and went north-east to Baracken north of Rocherath, where he prepared to meet his unit commanders as they pulled out from the Wahlerscheid attack. He issued oral orders designating a general defensive line east of Krinkelt-Rocherath then appointed Brigadier General John H. Stokes commander of troops in the twin villages and Colonel Hirschfelder as commander of the units in and around Wirtzfeld. At noon, Robertson proceeded to contact Colonel Mackenzie, commanding the 395th Regimental Combat Team to advise him of the general situation. He told Mackenzie to hold his present position (covering the northeast flank of the 2nd Division) until ordered to withdraw. He went on to indicate the general position to which Mackenzie would withdraw. Such a move would place the 395th Regimental Combat Team on a semi-circular bridgehead covering Rocherath to the north and northeast. A meticulous planner, General Robertson then set about controlling an orderly withdrawal from the Wahlerscheid salient. A message informed him that the veteran 1st Infantry Division was moving to his

70. General Walter M. Robertson decorates Colonel John H. Stokes soon to be promoted to the rank of Brigadier General.
(Courtesy John H. Stokes Jr.)

assistance. Initially, this extra support would consist of the 26th Regimental Combat Team, leading elements of which arrived at Camp Elsenborn around noon on 17 December. Upon arrival, the 26th prepared to move to the vicinity of Dom Bütgenbach, a cluster of farm buildings on high ground some 2,000 yards west of Büllingen. Standing astride Rollbahn 'C' at Dom Bütgenbach the 1st Battalion, 26th Infantry was to protect the south and rear of the 2nd and 99th Division areas.

In the forest east of Krinkelt, Major Mathew L. Legler's 1st Battalion, 393rd Infantry had not been as hard pressed on the morning of 17 December as had Colonel Allen's 3rd Battalion. The Germans had been content to move through the gap between the 393rd and 394th Infantry. Major Legler's 1st Battalion began its withdrawal about 11:00, having received the order to do so via the radio. By 14:00, elements of the 1st Battalion had managed to reach a position about 150 yards south of Lieutenant Walter J. Eisler's Company L, 23rd Infantry. A narrow front now existed east of the Twin Villages.

As a result of the initial confusion caused by the German attack across the International Highway, a considerable number of Major Legler's men, remained unaware of the battalion's move to the west. Among those who hadn't yet withdrawn were Sergeant Bernard MacKay and Sergeant Ben Nawrocki of Company B and Sergeant Lee Wilhelm of Company D. About noon, a runner informed Wilhelm's unit that they were to assemble in the former 1st Battalion command post area. Sergeant MacKay of Company B was still in his original position beside the International Highway. By mid afternoon, he and his buddies decided to vacate the position and likewise head for the battalion command post location.

As he cautiously approached the then vacated command post, Sergeant Wilhelm noticed a deer carcass strung up between two trees. Someone had obviously decided to supplement his canned rations. As stragglers wandered into the former command post, they set up a perimeter defense. The first arrivals occupied vacant foxholes as newcomers either dug their own or used such natural defilade positions as ditches to get below ground level. A forest trail that led though the position from the International Highway entered the forest at a place called Weisserstein some 600 yards to the east.

Sergeant Wilhelm's platoon placed its heavy machine guns near the trail in case of an enemy attack along it from the east. Once in position, these brave men prepared to meet enemy thrusts in the knowledge that they were cut off and without reinforcements.

Some 3,750 yards to the north-west, Lieutenant Thomas D. Brock of Company I, 23rd Infantry, called Captain MacDonald to tell him that German infantry were now within range. Scarcely had the call been made than a hail of bullets tore through the trees toward Company I. Guy Duren well remembers this initial attack against Company I:

> Perrine was pretty excited and I was beginning to think that things were plenty serious. The captain came by and told me I was to stay with him for Jackman wouldn't need me as long as Zewe and Hoffman were with him. Sergeant MacIntyre had come forward with him and the captain instructed us to start digging a good-sized hole.
>
> We got the hole started but MacIntyre asked me if I had any coffee on me so we took time off to brew some up. The captain had already sent

Perrine back to get a couple of men to help us so we weren't in any hurry until they arrived. Fuetsch came by and handed me a field phone and said to take it up to Jackman. I didn't know where Jackman was but started through the woods looking for him. During this time, considerable rifle fire broke out and bullets were flying through the trees. Doughboys were walking around upright but I wanted to crawl. I found the Company I command post and they told me that Jackman was up with their 1st Platoon. I located him in a foxhole. He had his radio set up and was evidently firing a mission for he was using his field glasses. He said he wanted me to give the phone to Zewe so I backtracked, found Zewe and gave him the phone then started back to the 3rd Battalion command post to find Fuetsch. There were two American tanks parked in the woods but I didn't think they could do much in the heavy woods and evidently they thought the same. Just as I got the battalion command post, Fuetsch told me they were pulling out to the rear. He had a radio at the command post and told me to get it and follow him. I wondered what was going to happen to my jeep but followed along. We walked about a mile rearward and I was thoroughly tired when we stopped. To our rear there was open country and our artillery positions were only about two miles further back. There were a couple of inches of snow and the walking had been hard.

Fuetsch instructed me to return to the old position; get the switchboard, jeep, wire crew and vehicles and bring them by road, back to the new command post. I wasn't sure I knew how to get back by road but hiked on forward. Doughboys of the 393rd Infantry were streaming back through the woods now and I was afraid I would be in no man's land if this didn't stop. I reached the old command post and found that the wire crew had already left for the gun position. A phone was still there on a line running between the Company I command post and our fire direction center. I rang Jackman and told him I had been instructed to move our jeep to the rear and wondered if he wanted to come along, but he said no.

At the time, Lieutenant Reidel fell out of the line of soldiers marching to the rear so I told him the situation and he told me to take the phone. He said he didn't know what happened to Miccioli, Hughes, Cobb and his helpers. Just at that moment, the Krauts threw in an artillery barrage. The shells landed about two hundred yards away from us, right where my jeep was parked. Reidel tripped over the wire and broke it so we had to splice it back together. All the foxholes nearby were filled with 2nd Division soldiers. Reidel fell back in with the retreating men and I sat there wondering if it would be safe to go and get my jeep or should I just walk back through the woods to the battalion command post. After about fifteen minutes and a conversation with a rifleman, I decided to go to the jeep. I made a dash and jumped in the jeep.

Guy Duren succeeded in escaping back to the gun battery position. At around the same time, Lieutenant Miller's two Sherman tanks withdrew to a new position just west of the woods. Captain MacDonald called Colonel Tuttle, his battalion commander, who told him the tanks were simply

71. An aerial photo of the forest north of Rocherath on the left, and clearly showing the Lausdell crossroads. (US Army photograph)

moving to a better position. Schulze-Kossens' 2nd Battalion, *25th SS Panzergrenadier Regiment*, made six frontal attacks against Company I. These attacks took place through thickset trees separated by foxholes. As wave upon wave of *SS Panzergrenadiers* came up the west bank of the Jansbach, MacDonald's men cut them down. Eventually, the Germans began making their way around the Company I left flank and the defenders began to run short of ammunition, so one of MacDonald's NCOs sent two of his men, Hugh Burger and Kenneth Lampton to battalion for ammunition. Captain Morris B. Montgomery, the 3rd Battalion Executive Officer, told Macdonald to 'Hold at all costs!'

At 15:30 five German tanks approached the Company I foxhole line firing directly into the shallow slit trenches. MacDonald called Colonel Tuttle and told him that without armored support, his position was untenable. Enemy small-arms fire killed Lieutenant Jackman and as the tanks reached a point some seventy-five yards from the company foxhole line they started pumping shells directly into the holes one by one. Realizing the hopelessness of the situation, MacDonald ordered his men to pull back and re-group

72. Private First Class Kenneth Lampton of Company I, 23rd Infantry pictured outside the R and R rest center in Vielsalm prior to the battle. Lampton was killed in action on the west bank of the Jansbach Creek. (Courtesy Hugh Burger)

73. *Rollbahn 'A' looking east towards the Jansbach in 1947. Photo taked by Charles B. MacDonald. (Courtesy Moire Queen)*

on a north-south firebreak about 200 yards to the rear. As they ran through the undergrowth, bullets zipped through the trees all around them. Once across the firebreak, they occupied a set of foxholes facing the dense conifer thicket through which they had just come. The Germans lost no time in attacking the new position. As he calmly set up his machine gun, Private Richard Cowan could hear the enemy officers' shouts and whistle signals.

Suddenly, Cowan opened fire on the approaching enemy and a tank round exploded above his head, temporarily stunning him. He quickly recovered and resumed firing his weapon, killing or wounding a large number of enemy soldiers following closely behind the tank. The Germans then directed three machine guns to fire upon Cowan. Undeterred, he loosened the traversing clip of his gun, grasped the handgrip and once more unleashed a hail of bullets at the enemy. As Captain MacDonald and his men withdrew once more, Cowan was the last to leave, covering the others until his ammunition ran out. Slinging the gun over his shoulder, he plunged through the trees in pursuit of his buddies.

Stumbling blindly through the trees, Captain MacDonald and two of his NCOs came upon Lieutenant Lee Smith of Company K. Within minutes, the Company K area was filled with smoke and shell fragments from exploding tank rounds. Once more, Colonel Tuttle's men reluctantly pulled back and reaching a clearing, they followed the forest edge rather than risk the open road through the fields in the direction of Rocherath. Among the taller trees, Captain MacDonald took refuge in a vacant foxhole and off to the southeast, *SS Panzergrenadiers* milled around two knocked out Sherman tanks. In an armored firefight, at close quarters, Lieutenant Miller's Shermans had

74. *Major General James van Fleet presents the medal of honor to Segeant José M. Lopez, a machine gunner with 3rd Battalion 23rd Infantry, in the Krinkelterwald.*

75. The two Sherman tanks of Lieutenant Victor L. Miller's 3rd Platoon Company C of the 741st Tank Battalion in which Miller and two of his men died just a few yards south-west of Ruppenvenn on 17 December 1944.
(Courtesy Pierre Dullier, origin unknown)

knocked out the lead enemy tank only to be knocked out in turn by the second Panther. Miller and two of his crewmen died in this engagement.

Private Jose M. Lopez, a machine gunner with Company M, 23rd Infantry, set up his machine gun close by Captain MacDonald's foxhole. Like Private Cowan, he inflicted numerous casualties upon the enemy and only withdrew as a last resort. Dusk was approaching as Colonel Tuttle's 3rd Battalion plunged through the snow-covered fields towards a group of farm buildings half way between the forest and the Twin Villages. Among them was Captain MacDonald, his overshoes full of snow, his clothes soaking wet, his mouth dry as a bone and longing for a cigarette. Back at the forest edge, known as Ruppenvenn, and later nicknamed 'Sherman Ecke' (Sherman Corner) by the Germans, the 2nd Battalion, *25th SS Panzergrenadier Regiment*, paused to lick its wounds. The unit had lost all its company commanders as well as its surgeon, adjutant and other specialists.

In the heat of battle that afternoon, Hugh Burger and Kenneth Lampton of Company I had gone to get fresh supplies of ammunition. Upon their

76. *Hugh Burger, the youngest man in Company I, 23rd Infantry. (Courtesy Hugh Burger)*

return to the company position, they found that Company I had withdrawn. As Burger bent down to examine an abandoned radio set, a stream of bullets tore into the trees just above his head. Separated from Lampton, Burger took off through the forest as shells exploded all around him. Suddenly, he found himself back in the place where he and Lampton had got the ammunition. He jumped feet first into a hole only to land on top of another man who was likewise seeking shelter from the incoming artillery. To Burger's surprise, the other occupant of the hole was a young *SS Panzergrenadier.* Both men jumped to their feet and pulling out a trench knife, Burger seized the German's rifle and with his other hand, made a lightning thrust into the man's stomach, jerking upwards with all his strength. He felt warm blood oozing over his hand as he pulled out the knife then swiftly rammed it home once more. The SS man's body sagged and he slid to the ground. A feeling of violent sickness came over the young GI as he wiped the knife clean on his pants then returned it to the sheath strapped to his boot. Summoning all his strength, Burger ran to the forest edge from where he could clearly see other Americans moving in the direction of the Twin Villages. Upon reflection, he decided to remain alone in order to present a much less obvious target to the enemy. Following a line of trees beyond the woods, he spotted a hedgerow and remembered how secure he'd felt when positioned behind such hedgerows in Normandy. In a final show of strength, he made a headlong dash for the hedgerow and upon reaching it, fell face down in the snowy field. Picking up a handful of snow, he used it to wipe the German's blood from his hand and arm. Suddenly, he heard a noise and quickly turned around to fire, but to his relief, he saw a fellow American soldier. Sergeant Willie Hagan, a professional soldier, aged thirty-eighty with eighteen years experience, was the oldest man in Company I. Together, the two men decided to make their way back to Krinkelt-Rocherath across country.

The German attacks against Colonel Tuttle's 3rd Battalion left its right flank neighbor, remnants of Major Legler's 1st Battalion, 393rd Infantry, completely isolated. Major Legler had no means of

77. *Sergeant Willie Hagan, the oldest man in Company I, 23rd Infantry gets a much-needed haircut during the unit's progress into Germany. (Courtesy Hugh Burger)*

communication left since all telephone lines were cut and radio communication had failed. As it grew dark, the Germans attacked the 1st Battalion, 393rd in force and Major Legler's exhausted companies moved closer together.

Seven thousand yards due east, Sergeants Nawrocki, MacKay and Wilhelm, and other stragglers of Legler's battalion, settled down for the night. In their hastily camouflaged positions around the former battalion command post, they adopted the password 'Wild West'. So as not to give away their presence they observed total radio silence and kept a low profile.

The 1st and 3rd Battalions, 393rd Infantry were by then totally disorganized, having withstood numerous enemy attacks on the east side of the Jansbach Creek. A few men had broken ranks but many others stood firm and were either captured or killed in action. Others like the remnants of Sergeant MacKay's squad were still to be found in their original positions some thirty-two hours after the initial German attack.

Chapter Eight

The 395th Regimental Combat Team withdraws

17-18 December 1944

In supporting the 2nd Division attack towards the Roer dams, Colonel Alexander J. Mackenzie's 395th Regimental Combat Team wasn't really affected by German attacks against the rest of the 99th Division during 16 December and the morning of the 17th. At that point, both the 2nd Division units at Wahlerscheid and the 395th RCT assumed that these enemy attacks were being made in response to their own push towards the dams. Major Robert W. Boyden, executive officer of the 2nd Battalion, 395th Infantry, for the period 18-20 December, later reported:

No information as to the scope of the German attack reached the battalion until late on 17 December.

Before noon on 17 December, word reached Mackenzie's command post that Lieutenant Colonel Justice R. Neale's 324th Engineer Combat Battalion, positioned between the 395th and 393rd Infantry, was moving back to the west. Companies A and B of the 324th Engineers had thrown down their picks and shovels and picked up M-1 Rifles to serve as infantry. In doing so, they forced the attacking Germans to detour to the south. Colonel Neale was moving his men to try and make contact with and cover the exposed flank of the 395th RCT.

The plan to withdraw from the Wahlerscheid sector resulted in the 395th RCT being attached to the 2nd Division. It called for Mackenzie's men to fall back

78. Major Robert W. Boyden, Executive Officer of 2nd Battalion 395th Infantry, who assumed command of the battalion when Colonel Mackenzie relieved his predecessor. (Courtesy Robert. W. Boyden)

79. Lieutenant Colonel Justice R. Neale, commanding officer 324th Engineer Combat Battalion, surrounded by his staff in Mürringen before the battle. (Courtesy Justice R. Neale)

down their route of attack in the direction of Rocherath. There they would deploy to defend the Wahlerscheid road in order to enable the 2nd Division to begin moving south from Wahlerscheid.

General Robertson ordered Mackenzie's 1st Battalion to dig in north of Rocherath on both sides of the road from Wahlerscheid. The rest of the 395th RCT took up positions along a perimeter facing east from the Wahlerscheid road and Rocherath, from where it could cover the 2nd Division route of withdrawal. Colonel Mackenzie then decided to send a messenger to General Lauer, his division commander, informing him of his new location and position of units. Mackenzie ordered First Lieutenant Paul E. Wells of Headquarters Company to carry this message. He showed Lieutenant Wells the situation map, and instructed him to commit to memory the map coordinates for the Regimental command post and forward units.

Lieutenant Wells set out for General Lauer's command post at Dom Ruhrhof, west of Camp Elsenborn by jeep and accompanied by his driver. On the outskirts of Wirtzfeld, the jeep came under enemy artillery fire and two 'dud' shells landed within twenty feet of the vehicle showering its occupants with mud. Further west, on the road between Camp Elsenborn and Elsenborn village, they encountered men and vehicles of the 1st Infantry Division, moving towards the front. Lieutenant Wells left the jeep telling his driver to follow him once the vehicles cleared the area. On his way to Dom Ruhrhof, the soldiers of the 1st Division repeatedly questioned him as to his identity as there were rumors of Germans in American uniforms said to be operating behind the lines. Upon arriving at General Lauer's Dom Ruhrhof farmhouse command post, Lieutenant Wells was again treated as suspect and nearly arrested by wary MPs. Fortunately for him, a captain from the Intelligence (G-2) section, who recognized him, vouched for his being a member of the division. Much to his relief, the MPs allowed him to speak with General Lauer to whom he gave his report.

North of Wahlerscheid, the Germans made no progress whatsoever as the 3rd Battalion, 395th Infantry at Höfen and the 38th Cavalry Reconnaissance Squadron, north of Monschau doggedly stood their ground. These units were well dug in with good fields of fire to the east. Having undergone the German barrage of 16 December, they were hit by wave after wave of attacking *Volksgrenadiers* of *Generalmajor* Dr Erwin Kaschner's *326th Volksgrenadier Division*. With artillery support from the 62nd and 196th Field Artillery Battalions, as well as elements of the 612th Tank Destroyer Battalion, they effectively stopped all such attacks. Reinforcements from the 47th Infantry Regiment of the 9th Infantry Division then moved into position alongside the cavalrymen and put an end to the enemy threat around Monschau. *Generaloberst* Sepp Dietrich, commander of *6th Panzer Army* therefore increased the priority on the German capture of Krinkelt-Rocherath.

Chapter Nine

The 2nd Division Pulls Back From Wahlerscheid

17 December 1944

On 16 December, two battalions of Colonel Francis H. Boos' 38th Infantry Regiment had passed through Wahlerscheid ('Heartbreak Crossroads') and pushed some 1,000 yards to the northeast. Their initial objective had been the eastern edge of the Monschau Forest, but shortly after noon, General Robertson halted the attack because of events transpiring elsewhere. Aware of the attacks against VIII Corps to the south, Robertson called Major General Leonard T. Gerow at V Corps to clarify the situation. Gerow told him that the commanding general First Army, Lieutenant General Courtney H. Hodges in Spa, refused to suspend the 2nd Division attack scheduled for 17 December and insisted that it continue as planned. On his own initiative, Robertson halted the exploitation on an intermediate objective. Later that afternoon the V Corps deputy commander, Major General Clarence Huebner visited General Robertson at his command post on the northern edge of Wirtzfeld. They agreed upon the advisability of halting the 2nd Division attack, and the possible need to order a withdrawal down the division's main supply route, i.e. the Wahlerscheid road. Huebner advised Robertson to go slow and watch his step, since the situation was not good.

Based upon direct orders, Robertson allowed the attack order for 17 December to stand and took the precaution of withholding the hour of attack pending his specific instruction.

In withdrawing from the Wahlerscheid salient, General Robertson intended pulling his units back though each other so as to permit an orderly move back through the Twin Villages to Elsenborn. He referred to this manoeuver as 'Skinning the cat'. As well as the main supply road, part of the withdrawing 2nd Division troops were to use the Hasselpat Trail which ran roughly parallel to the former. The two converged at a fork about one mile slightly northeast of Rocherath.

Colonel Mackenzie's 395th RCT was to provide cover for part of the withdrawal and, once this was accomplished, the 395th was to join the march back towards Elsenborn. The enemy forces at Wahlerscheid were by then so weakened that they posed no serious threat to the planned American disengagement.

The main danger was that coming towards the Twin Villages from the east in the shape of *227th Volksgrenadier Division* and the remnants of *277th Volksgrenadier Division*. The Twin Villages had to be held so as to permit both the 2nd and 99th Divisions to disengage and withdraw to the Elsenborn Ridge with the minimum of losses in men and equipment. Since the 99th Division reserve had been committed earlier, no additional units were available to cover the withdrawal. Delegating specific responsibility for various stages of the withdrawal to his subordinates, General Robertson nevertheless kept control of the overall situation. At about 10:15 on 17 December, he arrived at the 9th Infantry regimental command post in Krinkelt by armored car in order to confer with Colonel Hirschfelder and the regimental executive officer Lieutenant Colonel Ralph V. Steele. Shortly afterwards, Colonel Hirschfelder set off for Wahlerscheid to personally supervise the disengagement. The battle had now become a fight for survival by the 2nd Division. The same determination shown by its men on Hill 192, the Falaise Gap and at Brest would now come to the fore in and around the Twin Villages.

Lieutenant Colonel Olinto M. Barsanti's 3rd Battalion, 38th Infantry, had been engaged in supporting the 9th Infantry at Wahlerscheid. At about 08:00 on 17 December, Colonel Boos, the 38th Regimental commander, ordered Barsanti to move his men back towards Krinkelt. Immediately upon receipt of this order, Barsanti issued instructions to get the battalion moving south. He told his Heavy Weapons Company commander, Captain Holland W. Hankel, to get his heavy machine guns loaded on transportation as quickly as possible. This was expected to take about thirty minutes, during which Barsanti and Hankel, the battalion operations and communications officers, set out by jeep for Krinkelt. Once there, they could guide the battalion to its designated positions. The remainder of Barsanti's men were to move south on foot while enough of them would accompany the heavy weapons to place them in position and man them if necessary.

The command group left with Colonel Barsanti and Captain Hankel riding in the lead jeep. Passing down the dingy main street Barsanti's jeep passed the imposing stone church then drove southwest and downhill in the direction of Büllingen. Just uphill from a small bridge over the Holzwarche Creek, they passed a knocked out US 2½ ton truck which had been destroyed by an armor piercing round. The driver lay dead beside his vehicle, which had been heading in the same direction as the jeep. Colonel Barsanti decided that it was too dangerous to continue further and ordered the driver to turn around and back towards Krinkelt. As they sped back towards the village, a shell from a heavy caliber, high velocity gun passed close overhead. A glance to the rear, revealed a German Mark V tank, south of the creek on a bare ridge between Krinkelt and Büllingen. (This was probably one of the tanks knocked out by Lieutenant McDermott's tank destroyers later that same morning as they approached Wirtzfeld). Upon reaching the southern edge of Krinkelt, Colonel Barsanti met Brigadier General John H. Stokes, the assistant division commander and outlined his tentative plan of defense, to which General Stokes gave his approval.

At about 10:30, the Company M heavy machine guns arrived in Krinkelt and about an hour later, the rest of Barsanti's battalion took up positions on the east and south-east edges of Krinkelt. Colonel Barsanti told his men to look out for stragglers from the 99th Division who may well pass through the position. General Stokes attached all tanks and tank destroyers in the village to the 3rd Battalion with orders to block every road leading into Krinkelt from the east and south. By 12:30 there was at least one tank or tank destroyer protecting each such road.

The road from Krinkelt to Wirtzfeld had now become a bottleneck, through which all 2nd and 99th Division troops must pass on their way to the Elsenborn Ridge. Colonel Hirchfelder's 9th Infantry, leading the withdrawal from Wahlerscheid, was to concentrate the majority of its troops around Wirtzfeld while Colonel Boos' 38th Infantry was to defend the Twin Villages. Both Generals Lauer and Robertson thought it likely that the Germans would make an attack towards Krinkelt from Büllingen that afternoon. Fortunately no such attack materialized.

About 16:00, General Robertson realized that the situation north-east of Rocherath was deteriorating quickly. By then, he was well aware that Colonel Tuttle's 3rd Battalion, 23rd Infantry, was under attack by numerically superior German forces supported by tanks. Once the Germans emerged from the forest in force, they would be in a position to cut the Wahlerscheid road. Two of Robertson's rifle battalions were nearing Rocherath, having cleared the Wahlerscheid area earlier that afternoon. Lieutenant Colonel William D. McKinley's 1st Battalion, 9th Infantry, had left Wahlerscheid at 14:15 following closely behind Company K of the 9th Infantry. Before leaving Wahlerscheid, Colonel McKinley ordered his executive officer, Major William F. Hancock, to destroy all weapons and vehicles that could not be brought out. Major Hancock's men placed some thirty-five rifles on a disabled jeep and set fire to it before leaving. At 15:30, Lieutenant Colonel Frank T. Mildren's 1st Battalion, 38th Infantry, set off for Rocherath, following McKinley's foot column.

As Colonel McKinley's men made their way south, one of the men of Company A, Staff Sergeant Herbert P. Hunt, glanced to his left and right. Among the dense trees on both sides of the road, he spotted stacks of Christmas mail and packages awaiting delivery to the regiment. In the bitter

80. *A German artillery piece knocked out north of the Twin Villages. (Courtesy Robert A. Green)*

struggle for Wahlerscheid, Hunt had forgotten about the season of goodwill. The Christmas mail and packages would never get delivered.

The Baracken crossroads through which all withdrawing 2nd Division troops must pass, lies about 800 yards north of Rocherath. Three stone houses dominated the crossroads among the fields to the north of the village. Sitting in his jeep at Baracken, General Robertson halted Company K of the 9th Infantry and re-routed it east in the direction of the Lausdell crossroads, a junction of trails around a farmhouse halfway between Rocherath and the forest to the east. There General Robertson intended establishing a line of defense, thus protecting Rocherath against attacks from the east. As he supervised the deployment of McKinley's 1st Battalion

and Company K, an officer of the 535th Anti-Aircraft Automatic Weapons battalion walked up to the general's jeep. Captain Robert W. Bricker, commanding Battery A of the 535th, recalls this meeting in his own words:

I met General Robertson on the road north of Krinkelt. He wanted to know the type of guns we had as well as the number of men, equipment, morale etc. and where he could reach me. Talking to General Robertson that afternoon was a calming inspiration and his performance that day made all the difference.

81. *Captain Robert W. Bricker, commander of Battery 'A' 535th Anti-Aircraft Automatic Weapons Battalion. (Courtesy Robert W. Bricker)*

Captain Bricker's battery had eight 40-mm anti-aircraft guns and four halftracks with multiple 50-caliber machine guns. In addition, a plentiful supply of armor piercing ammunition, effective against anything but a tank, strengthened their firepower considerably. Battery A was attached to the 924th Field Artillery Battalion of the 99th Division. The 924th had been firing in support of the Wahlerscheid operation and was positioned east of the Wahlerscheid road just north of Baracken.

General Robertson met Colonel McKinley when the 1st Battalion, 9th Infantry and Company K reached the Baracken crossroads and gave him instructions as to his mission, apprising him of as much information as was available concerning the German attack. He emphasized the threat posed to the Wahlerscheid road, his main supply route down which most of the 38th Infantry and division transport still had to withdraw. General Robertson then ordered McKinley to proceed to Lausdell, take command of all friendly troops in the area and form a line of defense protecting the east flank of the division. He went on to tell McKinley of the units he had personally committed to the defense of Lausdell and warned him that elements of both the 2nd and 99th Divisions would be in the area falling back against the German thrust. Colonel McKinley was to stabilize and use such stragglers wherever possible.

Using two trucks that he had brought with him, General Robertson and Colonel McKinley set off with as many men as possible towards the Lausdell road junction. McKinley's executive officer, Major Bill Hancock was to lead the foot column to the road net as quickly as possible. By 17:00, Hancock had dispatched all foot elements and rejoined McKinley at his command post slightly northwest of Lausdell.

In the meantime, General Robertson had contacted Colonel Boos of the 38th Infantry Regiment, who informed him that the 38th's withdrawal was going to plan. The general then returned to his command post in Wirtzfeld. Earlier that day, he had directed the echelonment of the division command post back to Camp Elsenborn, the move being initiated around 17:00. At the same time, Robertson called V Corps by telephone to tell General Gerow that the only practicable solution was to stabilize the line Rocherath-Wirtzfeld-Bütgenbach that his division was now occupying. As a result of this conversation, the two commanders decided that the 2nd Division would hold and fight on the position designated by its commander. Units in advance of this line would withdraw through the position, reorganize, and then form subsequent reserves.

Chapter Ten

Lausdell-Krinkelt-Rocherath

Evening, 17 December 1944

Lieutenant Colonel William Dawes McKinley came from a long line of professional soldiers. His great-uncle, William, began his career as a volunteer in the Union Army, was brevetted to officer rank for gallantry in action and retired as major. He later rose to the highest office in the land, serving as President of the United States from 1896-1901. Colonel McKinley's father, James F. McKinley, followed in his uncle's footsteps and

82. Lieutenant Colonel William D. McKinley (3rd from left) and his staff from 1st Battalion 9th Infantry before the battle in front of one of the Westwall bunkers atop the Schnee Eifel. (Courtesy James F. Mckinley)

earned the Silver Star for gallantry in action. He ultimately retired as adjutant general of the United States Army.

Born at Fort Oglethorpe, Georgia, the young McKinley grew up on army posts and never considered any other career that the military. He trained as a cadet at the US Military Academy of West Point and the 1937 annual Cadet Yearbook, *The Howitzer*, listed *'Willie'* McKinley as *'Generous, tactful and jovial'*. Upon graduation, McKinley joined the 'Manchu' 9th Infantry Regiment of the 2nd Infantry Division, at Fort Sam Houston, Texas. As Regimental Executive Officer of the 9th Infantry, he took part in the Normandy landings. During the hedgerow battles in Normandy, he was critically wounded in an attack against a German machine-gun position but despite this serious injury, returned to duty two months later and assumed command of the 1st Battalion, 9th Infantry. Staff Sergeant Herbert P. Hunt, who served under Colonel McKinley, later said of him:

> He was a fearless and thoughtful commander; our welfare was always his first consideration.

83. Sergeant Harold Rutledge of Company A meets up with former Sergeant Herbert Hunt, by then a lieutenant, post Second World War. (Courtesy Harold F. Rutledger)

Little did they know it, but 'Bill' McKinley and his men were embarking upon the most crucial mission in the entire sector as they dug in around the Lausdell junction. Friendly troops streamed through the position from the woods to the east and north-east to the sound of heavy small-arms fire emanating from the forest to the east of Lausdell. Captain Macdonald of Company I, 23rd Infantry, accompanied by two of his men, met a squad of McKinley's riflemen busily preparing defenses along a hedgerow. Overjoyed at meeting fellow Americans, Macdonald asked what unit they belonged to. Through gritted teeth, one of the digging infantrymen snarled 'Ninth Infantry. It ain't enough we attack for five f...ing days. We gotta turn around and take up somebody else's defenses.'

Moments later, an officer of the 9th Infantry told Captain MacDonald that his battalion commander Colonel Paul V. Tuttle was in the Palm farmhouse just north of the junction. Making his way towards the house, MacDonald noticed McKinley's soldiers consolidating their hold upon the junction and its vicinity. Upon entering the farmhouse, Macdonald met the battalion operations officer, Captain Morris B. Montgomery who ushered him into the basement to meet Colonel Tuttle.

Out of the forest through Krinkelt recognizable landmarks 17-18 December 1944.

(1) Krinkelt church.
(2) Hasselpat Trail. Withdrawal routes of 1st and 2nd Bn/395 plus 2nd Bn/393 Inf Regt/99th Division 2/393 into position above (10 and (11).
(3) Wahlerscheid Trail. Withdrawal route of 1st and 2nd Bn/9th Infantry Regiment/2nd Division.
(4) Schwarzenbuch Trail. Withdrawal route of 3rd Bn/393 followed by 277th VGD and 12th SS Panzer Division.
(5) Weisserstein Trail. Used by some units to bypass Murringen.
(6) Jansbach Creek.
(7) To International Highway and Purple Heart Corner.
(8) I Co/23rd Inf Regt/2nd Div under Captain Charles MacDonald.
(9) 'San Souci' hunting lodge, 395th Regimental HQ for the 13 December attack. Later used as a German aid station.

(10) 924th F.A.Bn guns in position for the 13 December attack.
(11) 776th F.A.Bn guns in position for the 13 December attack.
(12) 370th F.A.Bn guns in position for the 13 December attack.
(13) 372nd F.A.Bn guns in position for the 13 December attack at Lausdell intersection.
(14) Tracks in snow show German tank park in forest.
(15) Ruppenvenn intersection. Area reached by 277th VGD patrol.
(16) Trapped C/371 and C?924 F.A. Bn snow-covered vehicles and guns.
(17) To Elsenborn Ridge and rear positions.
(18) To Murringen.
(19) To Wirtzfeld.
(20) Baracken Crossroads.
(21) Elsenbuchel Woods.

As he walked through the door, Colonel Tuttle greeted him with the words *'Nice work Mac!'*

Macdonald could hold back his feelings no longer and began to sob uncontrollably. His first major action, subsequent fatigue and flight through the dense undergrowth, had finally caught up with him. A cigarette helped calm him down as Colonel Tuttle told him that this was no local action, but rather part of a major German counter-attack against the entire US First Army. This action by the enemy necessitated an urgent withdrawal from Wahlerscheid by the 2nd Division.

In holding the west bank of the Jansbach, the 3rd Battalion had enabled the disengagement to progress as planned. Relieved by the fact that he and his men had done their duty, MacDonald left for an adjacent barn where some of his men were waiting. It emerged that many men from the battalion had made their way to Rocherath. Colonel Tuttle and Captain Montgomery left for the Twin Villages in order to contact Lieutenant Eisler's Company L. Once safely there, they would send back any men they came across from Company I. MacDonald and his men would then dig in to protect Colonel McKinley's right flank. Weary from the lack of a decent night's sleep, the young captain and his men fell asleep.

Outside, in a field just south of the farm buildings, the men of Company A, 9th Infantry, kept busy in order to keep warm. Sergeant Herbert Hunt sat in a slit trench, cleaning his Thompson sub machine gun and his prize possession, a captured German pistol. Hunt and his buddies had taken the precaution of lining their holes with straw taken from the barn. About halfway between the farmhouse and Sergeant Hunt's hole, Lieutenant Stephen Truppner of Company A crouched in his command post, an abandoned artillery dugout, writing a letter. Outside, Sergeant Hunt finished cleaning his weapons, lit a cigarette and sat down in his straw lined slit trench.

At 18:00, Colonel McKinley held a meeting at his command post, a dugout some 300 yards northwest of Lausdell, at which he gave all his company commanders further instructions and information as to the situation. He reaffirmed the importance of holding the position and told the company commanders to impress this upon their men. Companies A, B and C were in position across the trails leading through Lausdell. Company K was dug in around the Palm farmhouse while Captain Louis D. Ernst's Company D occupied a position between Lausdell and Colonel McKinley's command post. Although the heavy weapons company, this unit enjoyed the reputation of working as close as possible to the rifle companies. In addition to the 1st Battalion and Company K, a section of heavy machine guns and the ammunition and pioneer platoon of the 3rd Battalion, 9th Infantry, were in position around Lausdell. A platoon of tank destroyers from Company C,

644th Tank Destroyer Battalion was also acting in support of McKinley's battalion. The officer commanding these tank destroyers, First Lieutenant Raymond E. Killgallen, arranged to let the infantrymen have a number of anti-tank mines with which they could make 'daisy chains'. Tied in a 'daisy chain', mines could be dragged out in front of attacking enemy armor.

All told, Colonel McKinley had some 600 men positioned in and around Lausdell and, by 18:30, communication with the outside world was virtually non-existent. Lieutenant John C. Granville, the artillery liaison officer worked frantically to repair his radio set and eventually his determination paid off. Just then, Company B called the battalion command post to say that they could hear tanks approaching from the east. The GIs of Company B, held their fire until they could make a positive identification of the tanks, which in the heat of the moment drove past them in the inky darkness. In his slit trench, Sergeant Hunt sat smoking his last cigarette. He could hear the creaking of tank tracks but continued smoking in the belief the tanks were American. Suddenly, Hunt's platoon guide, Billy Floyd, poked his head over the edge of the trench:

'Do you hear those tanks movin' down the road back there Herb?' Billy asked.

'Hell yes Billy,' answered the sergeant. 'They're our tanks movin into position. They're the tanks we saw in the woods this mornin'.

'I don't think so,' Billy answered. 'They sure don't sound like our tanks. They're makin' too much noise. I think you and me better go take a look.'

'Oh, ok Billy,' said Sergeant Hunt as he flicked the ash from his cigarette and carefully stashed the butt in a crevice. The two men crossed the field and upon reaching the road, stopped and looked to their right, waiting for the tanks to pass. Suddenly, three Panther tanks loomed out of the dense fog, followed by about 100 *SS Panzergrenadiers* on foot. The enemy soldiers were moving along the narrow road confidently and seemed unaware of the fact that they were within the American lines. For Hunt and Floyd, there was no place to hide, nowhere to run, so they stayed put at the roadside feeling quite helpless. Sergeant Hunt could feel his heart thumping, as Billy whispered: 'Don't shoot Herb.'

Hunt couldn't understand how the enemy came to be behind the Company B position without a shot having been fired. He wasn't aware of the order to hold fire until positive identification could be made. As the tanks rumbled past, they splashed Hunt and Floyd with mud and slush. In the turret of one of the steel monsters, its commander gave Hunt and Floyd the vulgar middle finger gesture as he looked down on them contemptuously from the open hatch of his thick-skinned tank. In the cold evening air, the advancing *SS Panzergrenadiers* shuffled past the two Americans, scarcely looking at them. Now and then some of them laughed and joked as they moved west along the road. One SS man approached the two GIs shouting and laughing in German and got close enough to Hunt for him to note the foul stench of his breath. As soon as the last SS man passed, Hunt and Floyd raced across the road and bumped into another astonished GI. Stunned and shocked by what he had seen, Hunt asked the man 'Who were those guys?' The soldier adjusted the bundle of straw he was carrying to line his trench and answered, 'I don't know, but they sure as hell don't speak English!'

Moments later, as Hunt and Floyd neared Lieutenant Truppner's dugout, they heard the enemy tanks pull off the road and turn off their engines. It sounded as if the Germans were going to spend the night a short distance behind the Company A position. As the two Americans entered Lieutenant Truppner's dugout, he looked up from his letter writing and asked: 'What's up fellahs?'

'The Germans are up,' answered Hunt. 'They're right out here at your front door, gettin' ready to bed down for the night.'

'You mean the Krauts are behind our lines and don't know it?' asked the lieutenant.

'That's right,' Billy answered. 'The only trouble is our men don't know it either.'

Technical Sergeant Charlie A. Reimer, another NCO from Company A, entered the command post in search of ammunition: 'It sounds to me like we gotta chance to burn those Kraut bastards a new ass! All we gotta do is turn the company around and let 'em have it.'

'What about those tanks?' Hunt asked. 'How are we going to handle them?'

Lieutenant Truppner decided to call for artillery and mortar fire upon the tanks. While he made the call, the other three men would go back to the company position and turn the entire company around. Truppner was to wait about fifteen minutes before opening fire so that Hunt, Floyd and Reimer could complete the company's about face.

With that, Hunt and his two friends left the dugout and paused to let their eyes get accustomed to the darkness. Suddenly, as they started walking towards the road, all hell broke loose. The Germans opened fire with their tanks, rifles and machine guns and lines of glowing tracer fire raced towards Hunt and the others. Hunt dived for cover behind the roof of Lieutenant Truppner's dugout, as his two friends clutched at their throats and fell facedown in the field. He called out their names to no avail as both men were dead. From inside the command post, someone yelled:

'Who's out there?'

'It's me, Herb,' yelled back Hunt. 'Tell Lieutenant Truppner to get that artillery turned on!'

'We can't, our radio won't work. The lieutenant wants you to go back to Company D and call for artillery support.'

'Okay, I'll try,' answered Hunt as he watched the tracer rounds streaking over his head and into the farm buildings. In the barn, someone woke Captain MacDonald from a deep sleep.

'Wake up Captain, wake up! The sons of bitches have hit us again and are all over the goddamned place.'

Macdonald asked if someone had contacted Company L of the 23rd, only to be told they hadn't. Outside, Herbert Hunt made a mad dash for shelter behind the barn, which he then entered by a side door. As he paused to catch his breath, German gunfire peppered the front of the barn rattling its old boards. Above the din, Hunt could hear American voices coming from a corner of the building but he couldn't spot anybody. Seconds later, the barn caught fire so he darted outside on the last leg of his journey to the Company D position.

German tank shells exploded against the front wall of the house sending terrifying flashes of light into the night sky and filling the air with hot pieces of whirring metal. The Germans were still firing at the barn as Hunt raced across a field in the direction of Company D. Halfway to his goal; he slipped into a mud filled shell hole coating himself and his German pistol in mud. Wasting no time, he leapt to his feet and ran the last few yards where a GI of Company D helped him to cross a fence in front of the company position. Hunt explained the situation to Captain Louis C. Ernst, the company commander, who immediately took the precaution of establishing an outpost on the road between the farmhouse and Colonel McKinley's command post. First Lieutenant Claude E. Norman and Private Leroy Cates manned this outpost. Sergeant Hunt pointed out the precise location of Company A then gave Captain Ernst his best guess as to the location of the enemy. Within seconds, Captain Ernst called for and received artillery support. One lucky incoming shell penetrated the top of the turret of one of the tanks causing the ammunition inside the vehicle to explode spontaneously and blowing off the turret. The Company D GIs showered the Germans with mortar rounds as American shells passed overhead in the direction of the two remaining tanks and infantry. Sergeant Hunt borrowed a rifle and joined the men forming the Company D right flank from where he could see the Company A position.

Back inside the Palm barn, Captain MacDonald and his men hastily left the burning building and like Sergeant Hunt before him, Captain MacDonald sought refuge alongside the wall of the stone farmhouse. In the light from the flames of the burning barn, MacDonald watched as Staff Sergeant Odis Bone of Company B, threw a can of gasoline over a German tank, which then burst into flames. The noise of battle reached a tremendous crescendo and to the young captain the scene resembled a

84. Sergeant Odis Bone of Company B, 9th Infantry who set alight an enemy tank during the battle of the Lausdell crossroads. (Courtesy Bill Warnock/Odis Bone)

85. Lieutenant John Granville, a Forward Observer with the 15th Field Artillery Battalion at the Lausdell cross-roads, supported the 1st Battalion and Company K of the 9th Infantry. (Courtesy John Granville)

'movie war' He would later refer to it using the phrase 'Here was Armageddon!'

Like Sergeant Hunt, before him, MacDonald made a break across the field behind the Palm farmhouse in an attempt to locate Colonel Tuttle's command post. Eventually, he and three of his men, thoroughly exhausted, reached the Baracken crossroads north of Rocherath, where MacDonald found Colonel Tuttle, Major Joseph, Captain Montgomery and about fifteen enlisted men in the cellar of the Roehl farmhouse on the east side of the crossroads. Colonel Tuttle and Major Joseph had one K ration between them and insisted on sharing it with Macdonald. He hadn't eaten for quite some time and this tiny morsel proved a veritable godsend. Colonel Tuttle ordered the young captain to spend that night in the house after which he was to try and locate more 3rd Battalion stragglers.

Back at the Lausdell crossroads, flames from a burning German tank lit up the entire position as Lieutenant Roy E. Allen and Sergeant Ted Bickerstaff, both from Company B, heard the sound of more tanks approaching from the east. The two men immediately began preparing anti-tank mines to place in front of the oncoming tanks. They armed their eight mines, supported by one of Colonel McKinley's twenty-two bazooka teams, with the tanks about 400 yards distant. The two lead tanks rumbled forward as the soldiers of Company B held their breath and waited. Simultaneous explosions put both the steel monsters out of action and the other tanks in this column had to leave the narrow road in order to bypass their knocked out leaders. As they churned their way across the fields, McKinley's bazooka teams stalked them in the pitch-black darkness, knocking out another two.

At the same time, Lieutenant John Melesnick,

86. Lieutenant Colonel Robert Cassibry, Commander of the 15th Field Artillery Battalion of the 2nd Infantry Division. (Courtesy Robert Cassibry)

87. The wreck of one of the Panthers destroyed at Lausdell. (Courtesy Robert A. Green)

commanding Company B, notified Major William F. Hancock, McKinley's executive officer, that another tank column, this time accompanied by *Panzergrenadiers*, was moving west along the road towards his position. This column was long and appeared to stretch 1,000 yards to the edge of the trees east of Company B. Under the direction of Lieutenant John C. Granville of the 15th Field Artillery Battalion, gun crews of the battalion began to search the road with fire and their shells burst right in front of Lieutenant Melesnick's men, and then back east along the road towards the forest. This barrage continued for about ten minutes as the Company B GIs raked the enemy infantry with machine-gun fire. For

88. Two of the Panthers knocked out at Lausdell close to the position of Company A, 9th Infantry. (Courtesy Robert A. Green)

minutes after this engagement, the frantic screams of wounded SS men filled the air.

In their foxholes near the road, Sergeant Hunt's buddies spotted seven more tanks, accompanied by infantry, approaching their position. Once more, artillery came to the rescue and knocked out four of the tanks in quick succession. The remaining three continued along the road and past

89. President Harry S. Truman presents the Medal of Honor to Corporal William A. Soderman of Company K, 9th Infantry for extreme heroism during the defense of the Lausdell crossroads. (Courtesy Virginia R. Soderman)

Company A into Rocherath. Lieutenant Granville continued interdicting the road until ordered to stop, and the fire continued throughout the night. An undetermined number of enemy tanks were now within the 1st Battalion position only about fifty yards from the Company A and B command posts. Bazooka teams kept up their deadly game of hide and seek knocking out at least another three tanks and riflemen picked off the crews as they exited the knocked out tanks.

Private William A. Soderman, of Company K manned a bazooka in the vicinity of the Palm farmhouse. His loader had been wounded earlier, so he had to operate the weapon single-handed. Gritting his teeth, he waited patiently as a group of Panthers bore down on him, and then fired point blank at the lead tank setting it alight and forcing the crew to abandon the burning vehicle. Not wishing to suffer the same fate, the remaining Panthers withdrew towards the forest.

In an outstanding example of individual initiative, Sergeant Charles Roberts of Company D teamed up with Sergeant Odis Bone of Company B to destroy an immobilized enemy tank that had been causing havoc by firing its 7-mm gun point blank at the defending infantrymen. The two men got a five-gallon can of gasoline, which they poured over the tank then set it alight with thermite grenades.

At about 22:30, Company A reported a number of tanks deploying at the edge of the forest to their front. These tanks then approached the battalion from three different directions. The Germans had been using Lieutenant Granville's frequency and this forced him to make his calls for fire in the intervals between enemy messages. As the tanks began their approach, Lieutenant Granville screamed into his radio as he gave the coordinates to be fired upon: 'If you don't get it (artillery) out right now, it'll be too late!'

Battalion didn't acknowledge his request verbally but within three minutes heavy concentrations of artillery fire fell on the enemy tanks and by 23:15 the attack ground to a halt. The Germans apparently decided to wait for daylight before resuming a full-scale attack in strength. McKinley's 1st Battalion and attached units had not yielded a single inch and calmly set about preparing to meet the next push by the enemy.

At midnight, Colonel Allen of the 3rd Battalion, 393rd Infantry, arrived at Colonel McKinley's command post and McKinley told him to tie his battered battalion in on the 1st Battalion left. During the night, McKinley sent out several patrols to establish contact with the remnants of the 3rd Battalion but no such contact could be made. Major Hancock later described as 'frightening' an eerie silence, which descended upon the battlefield.

As McKinley's 1st Battalion and supporting troops had been digging in at Lausdell, elements of the 38th Infantry Regiment of the 2nd Division were still disengaging from around the Wahlerscheid sector. Lieutenant Colonel Frank T. Mildren's 1st Battalion, 38th Infantry, had

90. General Walter M. Robertson, commanding general 2nd Infantry Division decorates Lieutenant Colonel Frank T. Mildren, commander of the 1st Battalion, 38th Infantry for his part in the defense of the Twin Villages. (Courtesy Frank T. Mildren)

begun its withdrawal after the last unit of the 9th Infantry. Lieutenant Colonel Jack K. Norris's 2nd Battalion provided cover for Colonel Mildren's men using their mortars and fire support from the 37th Field Artillery Battalion under Lieutenant Colonel Tobias Eastman. The artillery fire proved most effective and Brigadier General John H. Hinds, the division artillery commander had reason to be proud of his men. Gunners of the 2nd Division Artillery battalions performed admirably on 17 December, firing both in support of the 9th Infantry and upon Peiper's column in and around Büllingen.

91. *Lieutenant Colonel Tom C. Morris of Waxahachie, Texas, Executive officer 38th Infantry Regiment. (Courtesy Tom C. Morris)*

On his way south from Wahlerscheid, Colonel Mildren met Lieutenant Colonel Tom C. Morris, regimental executive officer of the 38th Infantry who told him that the 1st Battalion was to link up with the left wing of Lieutenant Colonel Olinto M. Barsanti's 3rd Battalion so as to protect the east and north-east sides of the Twin Villages. Colonel Morris emphasized that Mildren's men might have to fight for the ground they were to occupy, a proposition that nobody relished. As Colonel Mildren's column reached a point just north of Baracken, Captain Fred Rumsey, the battalion operations officer, could see extremely heavy artillery fire falling on the crossroads. Artillery or no artillery, the battalion had to get through. Company A at the head of the column, passed over the crossroads with comparatively few casualties. The rest of the column however, came under a barrage of hostile shell and rocket fire and Company C, in particular, was badly mauled in what the battalion later referred to as 'The worst artillery fire ever experienced.'

With the coming of dusk, Captain Rumsey entered Rocherath at the head of the column, where guides were supposed to meet the incoming men at the junction of the main street with the road from Lausdell. Upon reaching the junction, Captain Rumsey met the sole member of the guide detail present, Lieutenant Robert O. English. The lieutenant was only supposed to act as guide to the command group and had never seen the positions the rifle companies were meant to occupy. He was, therefore, unable to offer any sort of meaningful assistance to Captain Rumsey, and so on the theory that it is better to do the wrong thing than to do nothing at all and hopeful of meeting the guides along the way, the column set off down the main street.

At this point, the battalion communications officer, Lieutenant Jesse M. Morrow, turned up with an urgent message from Colonel Mildren telling

Captain Rumsey to 'Take it easy' as artillery was breaking up the column. Colonel Mildren was on his way to meet them so Captain Rumsey held up the column to await his arrival. Some ten minutes later, the battalion commander still hadn't reached the head of the column, which the Germans were pounding incessantly with artillery. In the hope of sparing the men further casualties, Captain Rumsey ordered them to resume their march south through the villages. With shells bursting all around them, Colonel Mildren's men marched past the imposing structure of the stone church into the northern half of Krinkelt and minutes later, having come under small-arms fire, Captain Rumsey and Lieutenant English moved ahead of the men and met up with the battalion executive officer, Major Martin B. Coopersmith. The Major told Lieutenant English where he could find the guides and the column resumed its march. Moments later the guides appeared, but misfortune continued plaguing the 1st Battalion in the shape of accidents. An unidentified tank, moving down the street in the dark, ran over several of the men who'd been wounded by artillery fire and minutes later, a 2½ ton truck skidded off the road pinning four men to the side of a ditch. Despite these setbacks, the 1st Battalion occupied its designated positions, in houses and hedgerows on the east side of main street of Krinkelt and tied in with Colonel Barsanti's 3rd Battalion on its right and Captain James W. Love's Anti-tank Company to its right.

Lieutenant James Sturwold, executive officer of Company A, led his men

92. *Captain James W. Love of Anti-tank Company 38th Infantry standing alongside a Panther he helped knock out just west of the water tower in Rocherath. (Courtesy James W. Love)*

93. The Anti-tank Company command post in Rocherath after the battle. (Courtesy James W. Love)

into position just to the left of the 3rd Battalion. The move took place in cold evening fog, through foot-deep snow that covered the muddy ground. Captain Roy L. White, the Company A commander, set his men to work digging slit trenches to the sound of small-arms and automatic weapon fire in the distance. As the digging progressed, flares of a variety of colors fell to the northeast. As his men went through the now familiar 'Dig or die' process, Colonel Mildren established his battalion command post at number 41A Krinkelt, an abattoir across the street and just south from the church.

Between Company A and the road that passed the water tower, Company B under Captain William S. MacArtor, moved into the fields and hedgerows while Captain Ed C. Rollings of Company C and about seventy of his men, joined Captain Love's Anti-tank Company at the northern edge of Rocherath. During the march south of Wahlerscheid, Lieutenant Robert E. Berle's 3rd Platoon had left the column to establish a roadblock with elements of Service Company, 38th Infantry. The roadblock was about 500 yards along the water tower road at a minor junction where men of Anti-tank Company's 9th machine-gun squad were already dug in. The remainder of Company C, along with Lieutenant William Trumbly's machine-gun section of Company D waited in houses in town for about an hour in expectation of meeting a guide from battalion. As they waited, some men from Lieutenant Berle's 3rd Platoon and the Company headquarters who had been sent to the Service Company roadblock reported that they had just been attacked by

94. Captain William B. MacArtor of Company B, 38th Infantry who was temporarily captured by the Germans in Rocherath. (Courtesy William B. MacArtor)

95. First Lieutenant William D. Trumbly commanding officer Machine-Gun Platoon, Company D, 38th Infantry. Courtesy William D. Trumbly)

tanks and forced to withdraw. These men remained with the 2nd Platoon. Captain Rollings reported to Captain Love of Anti-tank Company and then placed his men in three houses on the west side of main street Rocherath and not too far from the junction with the water tower road. By then, in addition to the men of the 2nd Infantry Division, elements of the 99th Division, Company C and Reconnaissance Company of the 644th Tank Destroyer Battalion, 801st Tank Destroyer Battalion, 741st Tank Battalion and Battery 'B', 17th Field Artillery Battalion were in the Twin Villages.

Captain Rollings of Company C, established his command post in number 63 Rocherath (Maria Radermacher's house) and sent his 2nd Platoon under Lieutenant George S. Adams into a house on the west side of the street, number 65 Rocherath (Johann Drösch). Lieutenant Adams put one squad across the street into number 61 Rocherath (Johann Rauw). Company C now found itself occupying a position, which would prove crucial during the bitter fighting over the next two days.

In the basement of number 65, Johann Drösch, his wife Maria and their twenty-eight year old daughter, Hedwig, tried to get comfortable given the circumstances. The Drösch family, ardent anti-Nazis, had good cause to fear the return of German troops to their village. One son, Paul, had been an active member of the resistance prior to the liberation in September of 1944. Shortly thereafter, V Corps C.I.C. (Counter Intelligence Corps) appointed Paul Drösch mayor of the Twin Villages and Wirtzfeld. Paul worked closely with the American authorities and had regularly acted as guide to US patrols probing the Westwall defenses. Fortunately for him, he'd left the Twin Villages on 14 December to visit his wife and young son in Malmedy. The shelling on 16 December prevented their return so they remained in Malmedy, wary of what perhaps lay in store for the family members still in Rocherath.

Across the road from the Drösch home, two more civilians sought shelter in number 60 Rocherath (Richard Palm). The owner's wife, Thelka and a female neighbor, Suzanne Faymonville, tried their utmost to keep warm, not daring to leave the house for fear of being shot.

Covering the 1st Battalion withdrawal from Wahlerscheid, Lieutenant Colonel Jack K. Norris' 2nd Battalion, ran the same gauntlet of enemy fire as it approached Baracken. Colonel Norris ordered Company F into position around the crossroads and the three adjacent farms. Company E kept marching south and took up positions between Baracken and the Service Company roadblock on the water tower road. First Lieutenant Charles Curley, leader of the 1st Platoon Company E, watched in amazement as tracer bullets streamed out of the distant forest and across the open fields towards the Twin Villages. The fireworks he saw that troubled evening were far more spectacular than anything he'd seen as a boy, during

96. Lieutenant Colonel Jack K. Norris of 2nd Battalion 38th Infantry in white snow camouflage suit as the 2nd Division retakes the Twin Villages on 1 February 1945. (Courtesy Tom C. Morris)

Independence Day celebrations. Lieutenant Curley placed his men in a set of abandoned 99th Division artillery dugouts along a hedgerow. In the darkness, it seemed to him that he and his men were the only Americans in the immediate vicinity. Like other elements of the 2nd Division, Curley's platoon was short on anti-tank weaponry. At their disposal, Curley and his platoon had small arms and one bazooka with five rounds of ammunition. As they settled down in their soaking dugouts, Lieutenant Curley ordered them to take it in turn to catch what sleep they could. Curley's battalion commander, Colonel Norris had a different problem to contend with as he and his command group moved into Rocherath that night. At the height of the confusion Colonel Norris was trying to use his radio on its designated frequency but every time he tried to contact one of his companies, a strange voice would come on requesting directions. Eventually, frustration and irritation prevailed and Colonel Norris told the stranger 'Get the hell off my channel, drop dead and quit bugging me!'

As the 38th Infantry moved into the villages a few men from each company went east to give adequate warning should the Germans approach. One such man was Private First Class John T. Fisher of Company C, whose squad, along with another, walked east to a point near the water tower. These two squads were part of the 3rd Platoon under the command of Lieutenant Berle and were to occupy the two easternmost houses in Rocherath, number 69 (Ignaz Stoffels) and number 73 (Karl Andreas). John Fisher and ten other men went further along the road to establish contact with a squad from Captain Love's Anti-tank Company. Upon reaching the junction just east of the water tower, they positioned themselves in pairs along the roadside ditch. Off to their left in a field a US 57-mm anti-tank gun crew also lay in wait for the Germans.

After about ten minutes, they heard the sounds of approaching armor as a Panther tank loomed out of the darkness and someone threw a fragmentation grenade at the accompanying infantry causing pandemonium to break out. The Germans fired a flare and one shot by the tank put the US anti-tank gun out of action. A sergeant ordered Fisher and the others to move back towards the houses. As John Fisher leapt to his feet his ammunition belt became entangled in another man's equipment and running down the road, under a hail of enemy fire, the two men struggled to free themselves.

Once inside one of the houses, Fisher reported to Lieutenant Berle, who as an excess officer had assumed command of the 3rd Platoon when the regular commander died in the attack on Wahlerscheid. Fisher told Berle that the Germans had forced him and the others back and Berle decided to assemble his men and that he was going to a house across the street to make certain that all his men got out. As Fisher watched, Berle ran out into the darkness and a hail of tracer fire immediately cut him down. Sergeant J. Pepula told Fisher and his buddies to stay put and set off by himself in search of tank destroyer support.

Hardly had the sergeant gone when *SS Panzergrenadiers* appeared in the street outside the house. From an upstairs window, Fisher threw a grenade at the enemy soldiers in the hope that he and the others might be able to escape. The Germans fired a flare and a tremendous crash sent Fisher reeling to the floor as the tank fired point blank into the house. One man, Private Donald Foulke, was wounded in both legs, and before anyone realized what was happening, the enemy soldiers entered the house capturing Fisher and six others. Marching their prisoners outside, the Germans asked if anyone else was in the building. One of the Americans mentioned that Foulke was still inside the house and an SS man went inside carrying a machine pistol. Moments later, Fisher and the others heard a burst of automatic fire, after which the German emerged alone. The Germans then began questioning their prisoners, at the same time relieving them of watches, cigarettes etc. They demanded further information and when the Americans refused to cooperate, the SS men marched three of them behind the house and shot them. Minutes later, Fisher and two other men suffered a similar fate. As he dropped to the ground, wounded but feigning death, Fisher heard one of his buddies plead for mercy. The result of the man's plea was a further burst of fire followed by an eerie silence.

Lying in the snow, John Fisher heard the enemy armor and infantry resume their march into Rocherath. At the junction with the main street, the men of Captain William S. MacArtor's Company B were busy digging slit trenches when the Germans hit them. The darkness, fog and drizzle combined to severely restrict visibility and the incessant incoming artillery served to mask the noise of approaching tanks. The Germans began their attack with a heavy concentration of small-arms, mortar and artillery fire on the Company B area and as this attack began, John Fisher raised his head and looked around. Seeing no sign of enemy troops, in the immediate area, he set off across the field in the direction of the village.

The attacking Germans managed to penetrate the Company B perimeter and badly disorganized the defenders who then began falling back towards the main street. The Company C squad occupying number 61 Rocherath pulled back across the main street as their position became untenable. Captain MacArtor, his command post group and other Company B men fell prisoner or were killed. Most of the Weapons Platoon, a few Company D men without weapons and other troops, about sixty men in all, fell back under the command of Sergeant Carl G. Patterson and upon reaching the main street set up a roadblock just north of the church and the 1st Battalion command post. The enemy renewed his attack, throwing an estimated platoon of infantry against Patterson's roadblock.

Sergeant Patterson and his men repulsed this attack, but having no anti-tank weapons, they had to withdraw when German tanks joined the attacking infantry.

Patterson's group reached the church and dashed inside. Near the church the intrepid sergeant found two US tank destroyers, one of which he tried to put into position to counter the enemy threat. As the tank destroyer moved up the street, it received a direct hit and ground to a halt. Patterson lost sight of the second tank destroyer but he and his men managed to rescue two wounded crewmen from the damaged vehicle and evacuated them to the temporary aid station inside the church. At the same time, they also brought into the church, the Company B Weapons platoon leader, Lieutenant Robert Campbell who had been wounded earlier in the evening.

By then, the two enemy tanks near the church had lost most of their accompanying infantry, who'd either been shot or left behind. A few remaining *Panzergrenadiers* were riding the tanks which stopped between the church and Colonel Mildren's command post. Three Sherman tanks of the 741st Tank Battalion arrived in support of the Krinkelt defenders but the German Panthers quickly knocked out all three.

At that point in time, no real defense force had yet been formed to protect the 1st Battalion command post so an improvised group of command post personnel, clerks, officers of the battalion staff and Colonel Mildren himself would have to defend the building. Colonel Morris, the regimental executive officer, had been right when he'd told Colonel Mildren they might have to fight for the ground they were to occupy. The command post staff now found themselves under a mounting threat and their only available weapons were a light machine gun, a jeep mounted 50-caliber machine gun and an assortment of small arms. Across the street and just to the north, Sergeant Patterson's men had set the church up as a fort and they had a good view of the street by the light of burning vehicles and buildings.

Having dealt with the three Shermans, the enemy tanks turned their guns on the church itself but unable to penetrate its thick walls, they turned their attention on the 1st Battalion command post. The Americans inside the church and those in the command post raked the street with fire from both sides, pinning down the German infantry. During this stage in the fighting, Sergeant Grover C. Farrell, a member of Colonel Mildren's staff, picked up a light machine gun and stepped out into the street. With no regard for his own safety, he walked towards the nearest tank firing from the hip until forced to back off in the face of fire from the tank's machine gun.

As the battle raged back and forth, a wire team managed to restore communication between the 1st Battalion and the regimental command post a few blocks distant. Colonel Mildren asked regiment for tank support since the Germans were attacking his command post in strength. In the existing chaos, Colonel Francis Boos, the regimental commander, told Mildren that no such support was available and turned down his request. Fortunately, for Colonel Mildren and his men, the German tanks began moving away from the command post. It is likely that due to the light being given off by burning buildings etc. the tankers decided to move to a less vulnerable position.

Up the main street in Rocherath, Anti-tank Company and Company C had fared slightly better than Company B. Some fifteen minutes after two halftrack crews had joined Lieutenant Adams 2nd Platoon of Company C, one of the German tanks that had broken though the Company B positions began firing at the Drösch home. Down in the cellar, the Drösch family fervently prayed for deliverance from the carnage above. Lieutenant Adams left the house in an attempt to get a tank destroyer to fire on the enemy tank. Upon reaching the tank destroyer, Lieutenant Adams asked its commander to open fire on the enemy vehicle. After much deliberation, they decided that the infantry would fire an illuminating round to enable the tank destroyer to open fire.

Sergeant Andrew Paul of Company C had followed Adams out of the house. He removed a machine gun from its mount on a jeep parked by the door and, draping an ammunition belt around his neck, he began walking towards the tank firing the gun as he went. Suddenly, the gun jammed and First Lieutenant William D. Trumbly of the Company D machine-gun platoon grabbed the weapon to clear the stoppage. Within seconds, he managed to do so and took up the attack on the tank himself. An *SS Panzergrenadier* fired a rifle grenade at the lieutenant and it exploded against the wall, slightly wounding him in the leg. The tank fired six more rounds at Adams position then moved off down the main street in the direction of Sergeant Patterson's roadblock. The US tank destroyer moved out of the Company C position and did not return.

The Germans had also attacked Company C's northern neighbor, Anti-tank Company, taking prisoner several of Captain Love's men, including Sergeant Ron Mayer and other soldiers of the 3rd Platoon's 9th Squad. Moments before capture, Sergeant Mayer ordered his men to destroy their weapons so as to deny their use to the enemy. Upon capture, Mayer and the others expected to be sent to the rear as prisoners but much to their surprise, the Germans forced them to advance with them behind a tank heading into the village. Arriving at the junction with the main street, the tank came under fire from Lieutenant Adams' 2nd Platoon of Company C inside the Drösch house so it turned south down towards Krinkelt as the accompanying *Panzergrenadiers* hustled their prisoners down into the basement of number 61 on the east side of the main street. Adams' easternmost squad had vacated this building only moments before the Germans arrived.

After a few minutes, an *SS Untersturmführer*, described by Mayer as 'young and nervous', entered the cellar and excitedly told the prisoners that by New Year's Day the Germans would 'wipe the Americans off the continent of Europe'. Just then, from their position across the main street, Company C opened up with a tremendous barrage of small-arms fire, peppering the basement of number 61 with bullets, one of which killed an SS man. This angered the SS officer, who then forced Ron Mayer to go out onto the main street and tell Company C to surrender; otherwise the Germans would kill their prisoners. Mayer summoned up the courage to dash outside onto the road between the two houses. Using American slang so as not to be mistaken for an enemy soldier, Sergeant Mayer shouted at the men inside the Drösch home. Lieutenant Adams fired several shots over Mayer's head, Sergeant Mayer then made believe he'd been hit and fell to the ground.

Back in the cellar of number 61, SS men yelled out in heavily accented English for Company C to surrender, but their request met with complete silence from the American-held house. Moments later, from the windows of number 65, Adams' platoon saw three or four men in American uniforms, come out into the street with shadowy figures following closely behind them. Once again, the men in the street called out in English 'Captain MacArtor has been captured, if you don't come out in five minutes, they're going to kill us.'

Adams' response came in the shape of a volley of small-arms fire aimed at the shadowy figures and the entire group pulled back across the street. Sergeant Mayer lay motionless in the snow and in a further attempt to persuade Company C to surrender; a man came out of number 61 yelling, 'I'm from B, 38th...'

He stumbled over the word '*Infantry*', so Adams shot him for his lack of proficiency in English. Seizing the opportunity to escape, Ron Mayer jumped to his feet and made a blind dash to the nearest house. Unfortunately, in the confusion, he'd chosen to enter the very house he'd left some twenty minutes earlier. In the basement the SS officer told the prisoners that the Americans were barbarians who shot their own men.

Captain Love, the Anti-tank Company commander, kept busy all evening directing fire against the attacking enemy. As he moved between his squads, he marvelled at the use of floodlights mounted on the German tanks, which served both to illuminate targets and temporarily blind the American defenders. Captain Love later remarked:

> *The blinding light, followed by the inky darkness of the night in which nobody could see anything, made the battle seem as uncoordinated as if it had been fought in the pit. The enemy seemed to depend heavily on the effect upon morale of a high percentage of tracers in his ammunition.*

Captain Love estimated that most of the firing done that night consisted of one third ball ammunition and the rest tracer. Confusion reigned supreme as small groups of men fought each other in gardens, barns and houses throughout the Twin Villages. In moving around that night, Captain Love found, to his satisfaction, that, despite enemy penetration, the Americans still held onto the greater part of the Twin Villages.

North of Rocherath, Captain Robert W. Bricker began moving his anti-aircraft battery cross country towards Elsenborn. With Bricker's jeep in the lead, the convoy took a dirt track northwest of Krinkelt in the direction of Elsenborn. At the Wirtzbach creek, Bricker's vehicles became inextricably bogged down in thick mud and water amongst a host of abandoned US transport. Attempts to winch out the vehicles, using trees as anchors, failed.

Since Captain Bricker was under orders to get his men out, with or without their vehicles, he and they set out on foot towards Elsenborn and as he left, the Captain vowed to return and retrieve whatever vehicles he could.

As the 1st and 2nd Battalions,

97. *Lieutenant Colonel Frank T. Mildren of 1st Battalion 38th Infantry and Lieutenant Colonel Olinto M. Barsanti of 3rd Battalion 38th Infantry. (Courtesy Tom C Morris)*

38th Infantry fought to defend Rocherath and the northern part of Krinkelt, Colonel Barsanti's 3rd Battalion did likewise on the southern part of Krinkelt. At about 21:00, five tanks and infantry attacked Company K but since elements of the 99th Division were still passing through Krinkelt from the east, Colonel Barsanti ordered his men to hold their fire until advancing troops could be identified. As a result, *SS Panzergrenadiers* were within the Company K position before the Americans opened fire. The German tanks turned on their spotlights, temporarily blinding the defenders but Captain Davney D. Rogers managed to make a call for artillery support that succeeded in knocking out the lead tank. A bazooka team knocked out the second tank and the others immediately withdrew leaving behind their infantry who then became easy prey for the men of Company K who counted some fifty-two dead SS men after this engagement ended. These SS men were probably the remnants of the unit that had attacked Colonel Mildren's command post earlier that same evening. Two squads from Company K then cleaned out nearby houses killing eight Germans and capturing fifteen in the process.

In Rocherath, the Drösch family kept up their prayers, as soldiers of both sides played 'cat and mouse' through the dingy streets, where here and there, dense smoke gave way to bursts of flame as infantry squads engaged each other in hand-to-hand combat. The all pervading stench of cordite lingered in the air as soldiers of the 644th Tank Destroyer Battalion and 741st Tank Battalion sat in their vehicles up side streets awaiting the chance of knocking out passing German armor by firing at their flanks as they passed. In a face-to-face encounter the smaller US tanks were no match for the heavier German Mark IVs and Panthers. Inevitably, a lull occurred in the fighting during which men of both sides seized the chance to snatch what sleep they could. Captain Harlow F. Lennon, commander of Company C, 644th Tank Destroyer Battalion, lay down on the floor of the Faymonville house, slightly north of the church in Krinkelt which served as 38th Infantry command post. He had had a busy day and his men had done him proud both in the Twin Villages and at Wirtzfeld.

Elements of Major Mathew B. Legler's 1st Battalion, 393rd Infantry managed to make their way to Wirtzfeld but upon arrival there the battalion numbered only about 200 men. Major Legler and the bulk of its men including Sergeant Lee Wilhelm still found themselves stranded in the forest about 6,000 yards southeast of the Twin Villages. They had teamed up with Captain McGee and other men of the 2nd Battalion, 394th and were sitting out the night as enemy patrols passed close by their position. Sergeant Wilhelm of Company D lay motionless at the roadside

98. Captain Harlow F. Lennon, commander Company C, 644th Tank Destroyer Battalion at the Twin Villages. (Courtesy Harlow F. Lennon)

ditch as a German patrol marched past him their hobnailed boots grinding the earth only a few yards from him. As the night wore on, such patrols diminished, the Germans being equally confused by the darkness.

Colonel McKinley's 1st Battalion, 9th Infantry, and attached units at Lausdell, managed to evacuate casualties and received fresh supply of much needed ammunition. Throughout the re-supply operation, continuous artillery fire roared over their heads towards the German assembly area in the forest to the east. A wire team laid a line from McKinley's command post to Krinkelt-Rocherath, where signalmen relayed the messages to Colonel Boos of the 38th Infantry to whom McKinley's battalion was now attached. Colonel Boos emphasized the urgency of the 1st Battalion mission and told McKinley he must hold Lausdell at all costs until ordered otherwise. He also informed him that he and his men could withdraw sometime the following day.

At midnight on 17 December, General Robertson held a conference with General Lauer and Colonel Clarence E. Beck, the operations officer of the incoming 1st Infantry Division. They decided that General Robertson's plan of action was the only one possible, given conditions at that time. They would fight the battle in present positions rather than attempting an immediate withdrawal. The plan called for them to establish a reserve position along the high ground some 800 yards east of Elsenborn and bending back southwest to the village of Berg. The three men reached agreement as to boundaries and zones of responsibility and decided that the 2nd and 99th Divisions would defend the so called 'Elsenborn Ridge' to the last man if ordered to do so.

At 02:00 on 18 December, Colonel Boos sent a message to General Robertson informing him of the situation in the Twin Villages. The message read:

> *3rd Battalion holding steady, 1st Battalion badly disorganized, organizing local defense at command post. Enemy infiltrated with tanks and infantry on east part of Rocherath. Traffic jammed on road. Will put it through Wirtzfeld when road clears. Action quieting. Believe we can hold.*

As Colonel Boos' message reached General Robertson, Captain Robert W. Bricker's anti-aircraft battery stumbled into Elsenborn, the last element of their battalion to do so.

At 05:00 on 18 December, a relayed message sent three hours earlier, reached the 9th Infantry regimental command post in Wirtzfeld. It read:

> *To C.O. 38th Infantry: We have been strenuously engaged. Have knocked out three tanks. Others have infiltrated my position. Have situation in hand at present. – McKinley.*

Chapter Eleven

Mürringen Abandoned

Overnight 17-18 December 1944

By midnight, 17 December, broken elements of the 394th Infantry had withdrawn from their original positions, leaving Colonel Hightower's 1st Battalion, 23rd Infantry, in Hünningen, far to the advance of friendly units. American troops in Mürringen faced impending encirclement, occupying as they did an exposed position in advance of the Twin Villages and extending to the southern shoulder forming at Bütgenbach. Pressure on the defenders of Krinkelt during the evening of 17 December, made withdrawal from Mürringen a vital manoeuver. The 371st Field Artillery Battalion, firing in support of the 394th Infantry, ran out of ammunition and Colonel Riley of the 394th contacted General Lauer at 01:00 on 18 December, to suggest immediate withdrawal from Mürringen. General Lauer replied: 'Withdraw artillery, your order, your time.'

It looked to Colonel Riley as if General Lauer expected the Mürringen defenders to send off the guns and then consolidate with the troops defending Krinkelt. Riley contacted Colonel Hightower in Hünningen to inform him of the withdrawal.

Colonel Hightower now faced the problem of what to do with his vehicles, since it seemed that tank/infantry battles in Krinkelt made the road from Mürringen unusable. The dirt trails used by vehicles in summer were axle deep in mud and snow. The only remaining route out of Hünningen led though Büllingen, which Colonel Hightower knew to be in German hands. It looked increasingly as if his men would have to leave their vehicles behind upon evacuating the village. The initial plan was for the men to immobilize the vehicles by putting sugar in the gas tanks in the absence of sufficient incendiary grenades, prior to the withdrawal commencing at 02:00.

Shortly before the men were to start this process, an officer of the 2nd Medical Battalion arrived in Mürringen with the news that the Krinkelt to Wirtzfeld road was still open. Upon learning of this, Colonel Hightower decided to try and save his vehicles and gave orders for his drivers to evacuate them. The new plan called for the 1st Battalion intelligence officer and the motor officer to take charge of transport and they ordered the drivers to drive on until fired upon by small arms. If such hostile fire materialized, they were to dismount and assume firing positions at the roadside. From there, they would hold off enemy attacks unless threatened with the possibility of being overrun, in which case they were to abandon the transport and proceed to Wirtzfeld on foot. The order of march called for the 394th vehicles to take the lead, followed by those of Colonel Hightower's 1st Battalion. Foot troops were to follow and move across country on both sides of the roads.

Captain John S. Sandiland of Company D, 394th Infantry, took charge of his regiment's transport as the column moved north out of Mürringen. Colonel Riley rode at the front in one of the Headquarters vehicles. Constant shellfire pounded the road as trucks, jeeps and an assortment of transport moved slowly through the black of night then stopped on the hill leading up towards Krinkelt. Captain Sandiland continued up the hill in his jeep until it reached the southeast edge of the village whereupon he spotted a gun barrel and muzzle break, which he recognized to be those of a German tank. He immediately yelled for his driver to turn the jeep around and as they sped back down the hill out of the village, the German tankers fired at the jeep using their heavy machine gun. Upon reaching the column, the jeep ground to a halt where Sandiland met a fellow officer of the 394th Infantry, who told him that someone had given the order to abandon the vehicles and proceed on foot towards Elsenborn. Since this order was only supposed to be given as a last resort, Sandiland assumed that Krinkelt must be in enemy hands. Calling his men together, he sought verification of the order, which was subsequently confirmed. He sent a group of men east of the road to reconnoiter and protect the right flank while he took another patrol east and north.

Captain Sandiland had no idea of the situation or location of friendly troops but could hear the sounds of a firefight to the east. He and his patrol crept along a hedgerow where he fell head first into a foxhole landing on top of its sole occupant, an American GI. Sandiland was about to shoot the latter, when the man yelled out 'God damn!' This was what saved his life. The patrol had made contact with Colonel Barsanti's 3rd Battalion, 38th Infantry defending the southeastern edge of Krinkelt. Just then, heavy small-arms fire could be heard as the Germans launched a small counterattack. Sandiland and his men jumped into nearby foxholes and joined in the subsequent firefight.

At the bottom of the hill near the bridge over the Holzwarche Creek, Lieutenant William F. Kinney of the 1st Battalion, 23rd Infantry, had stopped his vehicles behind the abandoned 394th vehicles. The line of vehicles stretched right from the bridge up the hill into the village. Thinking that the Germans controlled the village, Lieutenant Kinney instructed his men to dismount and take up defensive positions alongside their vehicles. He then sent a patrol up into Krinkelt where it established contact with friendly troops. The patrol confirmed that a tank and small-arms fight was in progress in the village, but that Germans did not seem to be making much headway. The patrol discovered that the road to Wirtzfeld was still open and returned to report its findings. The drivers mounted their vehicles and every available man was used to drive the abandoned 394th vehicles. Enemy machine-gun fire knocked out two trucks as the column made its way through Krinkelt. At about 05:30, by which time the fighting had stopped, Captain Sandiland went back to the column's location to get more men to bolster the line but upon reaching the road he found the vehicles gone so returned to the 38th Infantry position. By 08:00 the entire vehicle column made contact with friendly units in the Wirtzfeld area.

Colonel Hightower's 1st Battalion withdrew from Hünningen leaving some 250 dead in front of the Company B position. The battalion left a small, heavily armed rearguard in Hünningen to cover its withdrawal and, as the wounded left by jeep, Colonel Hightower formed the battalion in a column of twos and began the march to Krinkelt via Mürringen.

In Mürringen, Colonel Douglas of the 1st Battalion, 394th Infantry, ordered his men to carry only vital equipment such as helmets, rifles, ammunition and overcoats; they were to dump everything else. In single file and with Colonel Douglas in the lead, the column set off along a heavily wooded draw east of the Mürringen-Krinkelt road. Among the men trudging through the slush and mud were Lieutenant William Vacha and others of the Company D mortar platoon who had fought so valiantly in defense of their position just southeast of the Losheimergraben crossroads.

They crossed over the Holzwarche Creek, tuning west along the draw then joined the road leading uphill into Krinkelt. Walking up the hill they passed abandoned 394th transport and stopped briefly as Colonel Douglas and his intelligence officer made a personal reconnaissance of the southeastern edge of the village. There they established contact with a heavy machine-gun crew of the 3rd Battalion, 38th Infantry. A guide from this unit took Colonel Douglas towards the 3rd Battalion command post but on the way they met up with Major W. B. Kempton the 394th operations officer, who told them that the entire regiment was proceeding across country towards Wirtzfeld.

Having established contact with friendly troops, Colonel Douglas returned to the foot column, where the men had manned the vehicles and were ready to move forward. He ordered the column to move out through the small-arms fighting going on in Krinkelt and the majority of the vehicles reached Elsenborn sometime on 18 December. The 371st Field Artillery Battalion was unable to extricate all of its heavy equipment and had to abandon all but five of its guns upon withdrawal.

The remnants of the 2nd Battalion, 394th Infantry and elements of the

1st Battalion, 393rd Infantry, still found themselves marooned in the forest about 3,000 yards east of Mürringen. Late on the evening of 17 December, Captain Robert R. McGee, the 2nd Battalion operations officer and his battalion command group, set off in an attempt to reach their rear command post. At a junction of trails known as *Auf dem Hergelt*, they ran into a group of men digging in.

McGee and the others stopped took cover and listened to the strangers talking. Soon, familiar GI jargon made it obvious that the digging men were Americans, so raising their hands above their head, McGee and his group advanced towards the diggers identifying themselves. It then emerged that the digging men were members of Company C, 393rd Infantry and that other elements of Major Legler's battalion were in the immediate vicinity. By then, it was dark, so the 2nd Battalion command group contacted the companies by radio (as indicated in the earlier story by Sergeant Harold Schaefer) and Captain McGee informed the companies that it was too dangerous for his group to try and reach them in the dark. The officers of both battalions then decided to join forces and move out together the following day.

Company K of the 394th Infantry, under Captain Wesley J. Simmons, was completely cut off from the rest of the 394th Infantry during its withdrawal to the west. At about 21:00, on 17 December, the cold, tired and hungry soldiers of Company K settled down for the night. They set up a tight defensive perimeter and planned to resume moving west at daybreak.

At about 04:00 on 18 December, a soldier from Company A, 394th Infantry stumbled into the Company K position, telling Captain Simmons' men he'd been captured by the Germans but had managed to escape. He told Captain Simmons that German tanks and infantry were positioned in a clearing about 400 yards to the southeast. A patrol, accompanied by this soldier went out and returned shortly to confirm this report. Captain Simmons made plans for immediate movement to Krinkelt, about 1,000 yards west of the company location. In the Katzenbach stream, 300 yards east of the village, Company K came under interdictory artillery fire, which Captain Simmons presumed to be American. When the shelling stopped, he and his men continued towards the village and upon reaching the outskirts, made immediate contact with enemy troops. Unfortunately for them, they happened to try and enter the village at one of the few points controlled by the Germans. Since it was still not yet dawn, they were able to withdraw to the south under the cover of darkness. They did so; unaware of the fact that most of the Twin Villages remained in American hands.

Turning southwest with Krinkelt to their right, they came across an abandoned US halftrack laden with C-Rations. Each man grabbed several cans and minutes later they sought refuge in a sand pit, as they ate for the first time in forty-eight hours. Their 'meal' finished, Captain Simmons led them cross country to Wirtzfeld.

By early morning on 18 December, despite German penetration of the perimeter, the Twin Villages remained in US hands, as did the Wahlerscheid road just north of Rocherath. Colonel Mackenzie's 395th Regimental Combat Team sat astride the Hasselpat Trail. Between them and the enemy to the east, Lieutenant Colonel Justice R. Neale's 324th Engineer Combat Battalion, made its way west under fire, both from the enemy and friendly troops. In the Twin Villages, the American defenders consolidated their line around the villages as they prepared for their move to the Elsenborn Ridge. Brigadier General John H. Hinds, of 2nd Division Artillery, by then had artillery positioned on the ridge within range of the entire front. From then on, additional firepower became available culminating in a tremendous capability of artillery firepower atop the ridge.

V Corps ordered General Robertson to hold his present positions until all stragglers of the 99th Division right wing had passed through his lines. Once they had done so, his units in the Twin Villages were to disengage and assume defensive positions on Elsenborn Ridge.

99. Brigadier General John H. Hinds, commander 2nd Division Artillery. (Courtesy General John H. Hinds)

German intelligence had failed to pinpoint the location of the 2nd Infantry Division and presumed it to be in reserve at Elsenborn. *Sixth Panzer Army* headquarters was not aware that units of the 2nd Infantry Division had taken part in the attack against Wahlerscheid. A result of this intelligence failure was that Sepp Dietrich did not expect his men to encounter much resistance once they had penetrated the 99th Division front line. This error cost him dearly in that his SS 'supermen' were by then, way behind schedule.

Chapter Twelve

'The Big Red One'
Arrives at Dom Bütgenbach

17 December 1944

The arrival of the *1st SS Panzer Regiment* in Büllingen on 17 December showed how exposed the right flank and rear of the 2nd Infantry Division had become. When US fighter-bombers attacked his column Peiper moved to the southwest in the realization that he could not remain on a route assigned to his running mate, the *12th SS*. A platoon of tanks did carry out a reconnaissance mission along the Bütgenbach road, but withdrew when guns of the 612th Tank Destroyer Battalion knocked out three of them just east of Dom Bütgenbach.

About 09:00 on 17 December, the tried and tested 1st US Infantry Division arrived at Camp Elsenborn. Elements of the division immediately set out for Bütgenbach, which lies on high ground just south of the Elsenborn ridge and sits astride the main roads leading west to Malmedy and north to Elsenborn. The 26th Infantry Regiment's mission was to

100. Troops of the 1st Infantry Division moving through Bütgenbach past the destroyed railroad viaduct. (US Army photograph)

occupy two hills midway between Büllingen and Bütgenbach, both of which overlook the road linking the two villages. Fortunately for the Americans, elements of *1st SS Panzer Regiment* jammed the road leading out of Büllingen thus preventing *12th SS* from making an attack towards Dom Bütgenbach.

By 17:00, on 17 December, Lieutenant Colonel Derril M. Daniel's 2nd Battalion, 26th Infantry, was dug in on the high ground just east of Dom Bütgenbach. The 2nd Battalion occupied positions along the reverse slopes on a 2,100 yard front with both flanks open. Colonel Daniel sent out patrols that confirmed the presence of large numbers of German troops in Büllingen as well as enemy vehicular activity at the road junction 1,600 yards due south of Dom Bütgenbach. (The latter was in fact elements of *Kampfgruppe Peiper* moving towards Möderscheid and Schoppen.) That first night of 17-18 December proved uneventful as far as the 'Blue Spaders' of the 26th Infantry were concerned.

102. Lieutenant Colonel Rox Rowie, commander of the 5th Field Artillery Battalion pictured with two of his officers at Bütgenbach in late December 1944. (Courtesy Rex Rowie)

On the morning of 18 December, small enemy detachments appeared in the vicinity of Dom Bütgenbach, but made no attempt to engage Colonel Daniel's battalion in combat. Throughout the night, the 26th Infantry kept busy completing its deployment. The 3rd Battalion dug in on the left of the 2nd and just west of Wirtzfeld, while Colonel Daniel's men remained responsible for covering the main road from Büllingen. The 1st Battalion, 26th Infantry remained in reserve around Bütgenbach as some of its soldiers dug trenches in the garden of the

101. Lieutenant Colonel Derril M. Daniel, commander of 2nd Battalion, 26th Infantry at Dom Bütgenbach. (Courtesy General Derril M. Daniel)

Villa Kirsch, formerly General Lauer's division command post. The 26th Infantry enjoyed adequate artillery and tank destroyer support.

In anticipation of a possible German attack on Bütgenbach, Captain Henry H. Kimberley's 560th Quartermaster Depot, named 'Truck Head 55', began urgent evacuation of stores from the dump in front of the church to a new location at the railroad station in Malmedy. The rest of 18 December passed without the Germans showing much interest in the 2nd Battalion, 26th Infantry.

103. Gunners of the 5th Field Artillery Battalion during a Fire Mission at Bütgenbach. (Courtesy Rex Rowie)

Chapter Thirteen

The Twin Villages

18 December 1944

The erratic German attacks against Krinkelt-Rocherath during the night of 17-18 December, had not achieved anything in the way of truly positive results for *6th Panzer Army* planners. Advance elements of the *277th Volksgrenadier Division* and the *Hitlerjugend* carried out these attacks in the darkness, against an enemy who was familiar with the terrain. By the morning of the 18th, however, the situation had changed in favor of the attackers. *Oberst* Wilhelm Viebig's badly battered *989th Regiment* had reached the western edge of the Krinkelterwald at Ruppenvenn and in view of the deplorable state of the forest trails, this in itself was quite a feat. The *Hitlerjugend* had made slow initial progress through the forest once committed to the fight, but by dawn on the 18th had assembled the *25th SS Panzergrenadier Regiment*, its *560th Panzerjager Battalion* and elements of the *12th SS Panzer Regiment* east of the Twin Villages.

Having first entered Krinkelt-Rocherath under fire in the darkness, the American defenders had reorganized overnight and were firmly in position by early morning. Most of the 38th Infantry was deployed in and around the villages along with a battalion and a half of the 9th Infantry and several platoons of the 23rd. In spite of the vicious German attacks against them, the GIs of the 2nd Infantry Division had badly mauled the attacking enemy. The Germans had superiority in numbers of tanks but General Robertson's men were determined to stop them supported by the few tanks and tank destroyers they possessed. The 9th and 23rd Infantry Regiments protected the division southwest flank in and around Wirtzfeld while Colonel Mackenzie's 395th Regimental Combat Team held the ground just west of the Wahlerscheid road to protect the northern flank of the 2nd Division in Rocherath. Withdrawing units of the 99th Division continued passing through the gaps in the line creating problems both for the infantry defending the Twin Villages and the artillery firing in support of them. Prior to dawn on the 18th, the majority of these elements of the 99th Division passed through the Twin Villages on their way to the Elsenborn Ridge.

At daybreak on the 18th, General Robertson took steps to protect the northern approaches to Elsenborn village when he ordered the 2nd Division Reconnaissance Troop and a company of miscellaneous stragglers to defend the Elsenborn to Kalterherberg road. Lieutenant Colonel Robert C. Cassibry's 15th Field Artillery Battalion also sat astride this road to help defend it against possible enemy attack from the north.

By 08:00, it became obvious how disorganized the 99th Division had become. General Lauer ordered the 394th Infantry not to withdraw to Elsenborn, but instead to take up positions alongside the 38th Infantry on the eastern edge of the Twin Villages. By the time this order reached Krinkelt, most of the 394th had already passed through town and therefore failed to comply.

Some time before dawn that same day, Colonel McKinley received orders concerning his unit's planned withdrawal from its position around the Lausdell crossroads. He was to begin pulling back as soon as Lieutenant Colonel Jack K. Norris' 3rd Battalion, 38th Infantry, was in position behind him and his men. In the meantime, they were to hold in position until instructed by Colonel Norris that the time for withdrawal was ripe. At daybreak, the enemy renewed his attack against McKinley's 'Manchu' infantry and as enemy tanks rolled out of the dense fog towards him, followed by *Panzergrenadiers* on foot, Private William K. Soderman of Company K began his own private war. Running along a roadside ditch, in full view of the enemy, he fired his 3·2 inch bazooka, disabling the lead tank and forcing the others to withdraw. On his way back to the Company K position, Soderman came upon a platoon of enemy infantry upon whom he immediately opened fire, killing at least three.

At around 08:00, enemy tanks eventually overran Colonel McKinley's front line rifle companies. Undaunted, the defenders fought like mad dogs to hold onto the crossroads, as two tanks left the road and ploughed straight through the hedgerow in front of Company A. From his slit trench in the Company D position behind the farmhouse, Sergeant Hunt of Company A watched helplessly as these tanks fired high explosive rounds directly into the Company A foxhole line. He saw men leap from their holes only to be mown down by machine-gun fire from the tanks. One man lay on the ground alongside a tank and jammed his rifle in between the track to try and stop the vehicle. All around the crossroads, hand-to-hand fighting raged, as the Company D mortar crews and machine gunners fired in support of their buddies. Six or seven men from Company B broke contact and started running for the rear. A report of this reached McKinley's command post via the Company C radio. Colonel McKinley left his dugout, personally met and stopped these men and sent them back to their platoon.

The position was fast becoming untenable with Company A practically overrun by tanks and infantry. Lieutenant Truppner informed battalion that he wanted artillery fire poured in on his own position since the situation was hopeless. He said that he and his men would duck into their holes and sit out the barrage when it came. This proved to be the very last contact between the lieutenant and McKinley's battalion command post. A thirty-minute barrage followed which stopped the Germans in their tracks for the time being. From their mortar position about 200 yards west of the farmhouse, Captain Louis D. Ernst's men could hear the familiar and distinct sound of GI weaponry begin to fade.

At about 10:00, Colonel McKinley received word that the proposed disengagement was to begin at 13:00 but estimated that without additional support, he wouldn't be able to break contact with the attacking Germans. Fate then intervened in the shape of the anti-tank platoon leader, Lieutenant Eugene Hinski who spotted four tanks from Company A of the 741st Tank Battalion and asked their leader if he'd like to do some fighting. 'Hell Yes!' was the tank Platoon Leader's short and to the point reply. Hinski directed these tanks to Colonel McKinley's command post, and with the German infiltration of the Company A and K position, McKinley reasoned that a counter-attack by these tanks might just free some of his men.

Down in the Company K position around the farm buildings, the survivors prepared to withdraw as more tanks were seen approaching from the east. In the full knowledge that elements of his company were still in close contact with the enemy, Private Soderman strode off to rejoin his buddies, his bazooka at the ready. In what was to be a repeat performance of his earlier exploits, he disabled the lead tank with one shot from the bazooka. As he ran for cover, a burst of machine-gun fire from the lead tank tore into his shoulder. Seriously wounded, the intrepid bazooka man dragged himself back to safety along the roadside ditch.

At 11:15, all available artillery fired to the front of the 1st Battalion position. This barrage lasted for about thirty minutes, at which point the American tanks counter-attacked, enabling Colonel McKinley's men to begin their withdrawal. As Sergeant Hunt reached the battalion command post on the left side of the trail to Baracken, he spotted Colonel McKinley standing at the roadside, grasping the hands of passing soldiers and thanking them for what they had done to the Germans. McKinley threw his arm around Hunt and said: 'Thank God, Herb, you got out of there! I thought I had lost all of Company A.' Sergeant Hunt turned his head to hide a tear. Most of the company was lost; the survivors numbered five or six men. As the withdrawal took place, the Germans kept hot on the heels of Colonel McKinley's men, despite the fact that the American tanks covered the movement back in the direction of Baracken. The rear elements were almost in continuous contact with the pursuing enemy as they pulled back. As Colonel McKinley and his executive officer, Major William F. Hancock left the command post; they could hear the shouts of '*Hände Hoch!*' coming from the enemy infantry behind the hedgerow. What was left of the proud 1st Battalion then passed through elements of the 2nd Battalion, 38th Infantry, which had by then moved in to cover McKinley's withdrawal as planned. The 2nd Battalion unit journal for 18 December contains the prosaic note:

> *13:30 Colonel McKinley's group (Index Red) had withdrawn completely and Colonel McKinley arrived at CP.*

Upon arrival in the Twin Villages, the 1st Battalion carried out a head count of its men. Company A had five, Company B had twenty-seven, Company C had forty, Company D numbered sixty and Company K was down to twelve. Only 144 of the original 600 men made it out of Lausdell, the remnants were barely sufficient to form six rifle squads. On 30 December 1944 the *New York Times* printed the following article by one of its correspondents, Harold Denny:

> *By the gallantry of one battalion, a regiment was saved; and so on until the heroism of this one battalion had pyramided into a victorious defense at the precise point where the Germans had expected to break clear through our lines, cut the Allies' armies in two and inflict a devastating defeat. This battalion played a crucial role in averting a disastrous defeat in this greatest battle in American history.'**

Once through the Lausdell crossroads, the Germans attacked Rocherath with renewed vigor on the morning of the 18th. Just after daylight, at about 08:00, five tanks with infantry riding on the first three, came along the water tower road towards the main road. Captain Harlow F. Lennon and the men of his Company C, 644th Tank Destroyer Battalion, were ready and waiting to do battle as were the tankers of the 741st Tank Battalion. As the first tank passed in front of Colonel Boos' command post, one of Captain Lennon's tank destroyers, only fifty yards from the building, opened fire knocking it out. The enemy column stopped and Lennon's men finished off the second and third tanks in line as SS squad leaders yelled for their men to jump off the vehicles. From the windows of their command post in the Faymonville house just west of the main street, Colonel Boos' men fired every weapon at hand at the enemy and few of them escaped. A bazooka team from Company A, 38th Infantry, in position near the command post, knocked out the fourth tank while a tank destroyer fired at the fifth but failed to put it out of action. Apparently, deciding that discretion was the better part of valor, the enemy tank then pulled out of the area.

In their 'fortress' facing the water tower road, Lieutenant George S. Adams' 2nd Platoon of Company C, began the morning sniping at any

Germans who dared show themselves in the windows of the Rauw house across the main street. Just before 09:00, Captain Rollings and his runner dashed safely past the enemy held house into the Drösch home and upon learning that the enemy had captured number 61 across the street, Captain Rollings ordered Lieutenant Adams to recapture the building.

Covered by a volley of rifle shots, Adams' 2nd Squad attacked across the narrow main street and as Captain Rollings stood watching them, from the doorway of number 65, a ricocheting bullet struck him in the leg. A wounded SS man in the basement of the Rauw house (number 61) threw a grenade into the street, wounding two of Lieutenant Adams' men. The Germans fired two flares, soon after which tanks could be heard approaching from the direction of Lausdell. Nevertheless, the Americans recaptured number 61, killing eleven Germans and taking about twenty prisoners. Down in the basement, Adams' men released Lieutenant Ralph L. Schmidt of Company B, Sergeant Ron Mayer of Anti-tank Company and other men of the 1st Battalion, all of whom the Germans had captured earlier. The released Americans picked up what weapons they could find collected ammunition from an abandoned US halftrack then set out in search of their respective units. Among the wounded German prisoners were two who could speak some English, so Adams' men took them across to the Drösch home while Captain Rollings and his runner took away the rest.

In position about 100 yards north of Lieutenant Adams' 2nd Platoon of Company C, men of Captain James W. Love's Anti-tank Company in the company command post could hear the approaching enemy armor. Captain Love wondered how these tanks had got past his 5th Squad and immediately informed regiment of the situation. As he did so, about eight enemy tanks burst into view racing at top speed past the water tower towards the main street. Prior to reaching the road junction with the main street, they slowed then stopped with the lead vehicle about fifty yards from the junction and some 200 yards across the field from the anti-tank command post. Captain Love left the command post and found two self-propelled tank destroyers in a good position to knock out the enemy tanks providing they would move but a few yards. Upon asking the crews to do so, they refused, saying that they were under orders to stay put, covering vital positions. Determined to stop this enemy push, Captain Love then located an American M-4 tank and led it into a position from where it could fire upon the enemy armor. As he did so, another enemy tank, this time a Mark 3, fired its co-axial machine gun at him, one of the bullets glancing off his helmet. Two perfect flanking shots into the side of the Panther put it out of action. As the crew baled out, the Anti-tank Company soldiers picked them off from the upstairs windows of the command post. The remaining tanks began moving forward and then stopped to the rear of number 61. Sergeant Richard Shinefelt, in charge of Lieutenant Adams' 2nd Squad, occupying number 61, fired a couple of rifle grenades at the enemy tanks without any apparent effect. The 2nd Platoon riflemen in both houses, fired at enemy infantry, riding the tanks, killing or wounding them all.

Minutes later, a supply of bazooka ammunition reached the Anti-tank Company position much to the relief of the defenders. Soon another Panther began moving along the road past the water tower. Private Isabel Salazar, a cook's helper, grabbed a bazooka and ran upstairs to one of the command post first floor windows. From this new vantage point, he knocked out the enemy tank with one rocket and the momentum of the tank carried it forward into position alongside the one knocked out earlier by the M-4 tank. Personnel in the Company C command post, managed to put another tank out of action and shortly afterwards Private Salazar gave a repeat performance by knocking out a 75mm *Jagdpanzer* (tank destroyer) that had pulled up behind the two Panthers. Three of the enemy tanks pulled up at the junction with the main street, one facing south towards Krinkelt, a second due west and the third northwest towards the Drösch house. This third tank then fired one shot at the house that only succeeded in shaking plaster loose from the walls. Down in the basement, the Drösch family, some neighbors who'd joined them and the two SS prisoners felt the building tremble. Through a rear window on the ground floor, Lieutenant Adams' men could clearly see US tanks and tank destroyers moving into position just north of them up the main street. A large-scale tank battle was about to break out in the immediate vicinity. Adams and his men left the building and moved slightly north to a house next to the Anti-tank Company command post while the two prisoners and the civilians remained in the cellar of number 65.

Moments after the 2nd Platoon left the building, heavy gunfire tore the air apart as Panthers, Shermans and US tank destroyers engaged each other in combat. Elsewhere in the Twin Villages, infantrymen of both sides fought viciously for control of the various buildings. In Krinkelt, a medic from the 99th Division came into the Company A front line on the eastern edge of the village. A suspicious GI stopped the man and sent him to the Company A, 38th Infantry command post under guard for questioning by the command post staff. They verified his identity as an American soldier and he told them that the Germans were holding about 150 US prisoners on the reverse slope of a hill known as the Enkelberg which lies about 800 yards southeast of the village and just west of the Mürringen to Krinkelt road. American artillery was shelling the road and the Germans had sent this medic into the village to ask the defenders to surrender. He told his interrogators that he'd seen about 200 enemy soldiers and that they were without tank support. The Company A radio operator contacted the 1st Battalion command post and shortly thereafter, the US artillery fire increased. The sounds of frantic digging and chopping followed this more intense shelling as the Germans sought whatever shelter they could.

Uphill in Krinkelt, Colonel Mildren's command post also came under renewed attack on the morning of the 18th. This time, however, the command post staff was better prepared than it had been the previous evening. Across the street, just to the north, Sergeant Patterson's group still held the battered stone church. At daylight, Lieutenant Sidney P. Dane, the 1st Battalion intelligence officer, crossed the road and stood outside the church, which he believed to be held by the Germans. He called out in German, (of which none of Sergeant Patterson's men understood a single word) for the men inside to give up. Getting no response, he then yelled out in English and told the men inside who he was. Sergeant Patterson's men emerged from the imposing stone structure and under Lieutenant Dane's guidance reported to the battalion command post where they picked up bazookas and took up defensive positions east and northeast of the building.

Early that same morning, *Oberstleutnant* Gerhard Lemcke, commanding the *89th Fusilier Regiment* of *12th Volksgrenadier Division*, ordered his *1st Battalion*, under *Hauptman* Ripke to move into Mürringen. Shortly thereafter, *Oberstleutnant* Lemcke himself decided to enter the village. Climbing into a captured US jeep, he and three of his men drove west along Rollbahn 'C' in the direction of Büllingen. Lemcke's driver missed the first right turn into the village and continued driving west along the main road. Realizing his mistake, Lemcke ordered the driver to take the next turn, approaching Mürringen from the southwest. As they drove up the hillside into the village, Lemcke stood upright in the jeep waving his officer's cap and shouting in German so that Ripke's men wouldn't mistake the approaching men for American soldiers. In the center of the village, which was badly damaged by artillery fire, Lemcke spoke with *Hauptman* Ripke who told him that his men had entered the village without meeting enemy troops. Two civilians showed the Germans the location of buildings, which had housed the US command posts. Ripke told Lemcke that he believed some enemy soldiers might still be in position somewhere in the forest to the east.

At 09:30, those same Americans began moving west. Captain McGee, Major Legler, Sergeant Schaefer and others of the 1st Battalion, 393rd and 2nd Battalion, 394th reached the edge of the forest and stopped in an attempt to make radio contact with friendly forces. After several such attempts they met with success on their fast-fading radio set. Using a kind of veiled double talk and by means of code, they identified themselves and asked their contact for information about friendly dispositions. Since their radio signal was very weak, they arranged for their contact to call back in fifteen minutes, by which time they would switch the radio back on again. When they eventually re-established contact, the contact informed them that the nearest friendly troops were in Krinkelt. The entire conversation took place in guarded terms, since they suspected that the Germans might be using captured radio sets. At the sight of a German tank heading for Krinkelt, Captain McGee, and the others decided to head for Mürringen.

The 2nd Battalion, 394th, moved out first with Major Legler's 1st Battalion, 393rd bringing up the rear. Sergeant Harold Schaefer of the 2nd Platoon, Company G, 394th later wrote his memories of that morning's attempt to enter Mürringen:

> *Around mid morning, the lead elements encountered Jerry troops and had a brief exchange of small arms fire. Contact was broken off and they did not chase us. There were more than enough of them to give chase but they were attacking the Twin Villages so had their own mission to accomplish. It was then decided to head for Mürringen where regiment had been and at about 12:30, we came out of the forest on a logging trail (Rollbahn 'B'). There was a bridge over the Holzwarche creek but I didn't use it because Company G fanned out to the left of the trail, while Companies E and F proceeded on the right. According to a Company E survivor, they advanced to a reservoir on the Dickesknipp where they came under heavy fire and got pinned down. We were oblivious of this and continued towards Mürringen. As we did, we had the opportunity to restock our packs with rations we found in abandoned foxholes. We must have been nuts to think that regiment was in Mürringen when these defenses (the foxholes) were vacated, so why we went in there is a mystery! Captain Haymaker was a good commanding officer but a bit over zealous in this case. First, Company G had lost contact with Company E, so both flanks were exposed. Second, the town was not defended by U.S. troops, and third, we attacked with no heavy weapons support.*

Sergeant Schaefer made it up the hill and took part in the capture of the first two houses upon entering the village. Schaefer's 1st Squad then crossed the road in an attempt to make contact with Company E and as he proceeded down a hedgerow, Sergeant Schaefer met his first German face on and made him die for his country. He then met men of the 3rd Squad but no one from Company E. On his way back to the road he came across a man called Jurgill lying seriously wounded by the hedgerow. Schaefer made it across the road to the first house where he reported to his company commander Captain John N. Haymaker who ordered Schaefer and another man to bring back Jurgill, which they then accomplished in spite of heavy incoming machine-gun fire. Shortly after this, outside of the house, Schaefer witnessed a heated discussion involving members of the command staff and during which someone mentioned the possibility of surrender. Sergeant Schaefer had no intention of surrendering so decided that rather than surrendering, he for one would head back east into the forest.

104. Sergeant William C. White – Assistant Squad Leader, 2nd Squad, 2nd Platoon, Company G, 394th Infantry. (Courtesy William C. White)

Meanwhile, Captain Haymaker ordered Lieutenant James C. Burtner's 2nd platoon of Company G to enter the village in order to ascertain who in fact held it. Lieutenant Burtner led his 2nd Squad along with part of the 1st Platoon, past the first two houses on the left into the village. Lieutenant Burtner's group then passed behind the second house, a large stone structure and raced across a road to the shelter of a stone barn. Sergeant William C. White served as the assistant leader of Burtner's 2nd Squad as it crossed the road under German machine-gun fire. As Sergeant White tried to position his BAR close by the corner of the barn, the Germans spotted him and fired a mortar round which exploded wounding him slightly in the arm. Luckily for him, his heavy greatcoat helped cushion the effect of the mortar round and Sergeant James W. Hill, his squad leader, helped him roll up his sleeve to inspect the wound. The two men followed their buddies inside the barn as German soldiers across the road raked the building with fire. Inside, incoming machine-gun bullets ricocheted off the walls hitting men and cattle alike, as Sergeant White struggled to bandage his arm. Lieutenant Burtner and Technical Sergeant D. Rush decided to try and make it back across the road. Lieutenant Burtner made it across but Sergeant Rush died in a hail of German machine-gun fire. The Germans then began throwing grenades into the building as well as mortar rounds and it soon became evident that the situation was hopeless. The choice was simple, either stay in the barn and be killed or opt for surrender. Sergeant Whiteley, the ranking NCO then stepped to the doorway and yelled 'Kamarad' at the top of his voice. German infantrymen with bayonets fixed then moved in to capture the GIs who'd already lain down their weapons and raised their hands in surrender.

Back at the edge of the village, Sergeant Schaefer and the rest of the battalion prepared to leave. Sergeant Schaefer's story continues:

We left Mürringen around 16:00 hours with a beautiful fog covering our withdrawal. We had left some 30 able bodied and 15 wounded. Not a good three hours. In return, we had one prisoner, an ox of a man and looking twice his size in his greatcoat. He was very helpful in bringing out our wounded. Our retreat from Mürringen took us on a path four hundred yards in front of where Company E was pinned down. I can't to this day figure out why these Germans didn't fire on us.

We assembled in an area of safety near Company E and got the word that Company F and Captain John H. Goodner were going to lead us out. While waiting, we decided that our Sergeant Reynolds, who had been shot through the mouth, should be surrendered for medical aid. Harvey Williams volunteered to take his buddy back using an abandoned jeep we found in the assembly area. The Germans refused them and before we left, here came Harvey, Reynolds and the jeep. Frank walked it out helped by Williams, Rump and others. Essentially, we were to follow the Holzwarche draw or valley through Wirtzfeld. Some of us did and others didn't.

In Rocherath, other civilians, including Joseph Schroeder, his sisters Hedwig and Mathilde, Alex Kreutz, Sophie Faymonville and Anna Hoenen, had joined the Drösch family in the basement of number 65. Across the street in number 60, Thekla Palm and Susanne Faymonville had cause for worry. Late that morning, an SS officer and his men entered the house. On the opposite side of the street at an attic window in number 63, a soldier wearing a German helmet, beckoned the SS men across the road. The SS officer left the house and walked out into the street. Suddenly, the man in number 63 opened fire, knocking off the German's glasses and wounding him in the hand as he dashed into a nearby barn. Back at number 60, his men threatened to shoot the two women if their officer couldn't be found. At that moment, he re-appeared, nursing his wounded hand and carrying his glasses. He politely asked if the women could bandage his bleeding hand and as they did so, he asked them: 'How can I get out of this hell?'

They told him and his men left. Minutes later, Lieutenant Adams' platoon re-occupied number 65 and as Thekla Palm looked out of her door, one of Adams' men waved her and Susanne across the street. Not wishing to remain alone, the two women raced across the road to join the other civilians in the basement of number 65.

His return to the platoon position reminded Adams that he'd left his two prisoners in the basement. One of them, an officer, had a serious leg wound; the other, an enlisted man, was less severely injured. The officer was still in the basement when Adams went downstairs, but the enlisted man had

No

Nam ..... Drösch.

Prénom ..... Paul

Secteur ..... Pts

Fonction ..... Ag d R.

Ce document strictement confidentiel. A tenir à l'abri des perquisitions.

Date de délivrance:
1. 7. 42

Signature du porte

Liège, le 1er juillet 4..

Signature de la Direction, ..

SERVICE

105. The identity card showing Paul Drösch, the US appointed burgomaster of the Twin Villages to have been an active member of the Belgian resistance. (Courtesy Paul Drösch) vanished. Adams ran back upstairs in the hope of spotting the man. Sure enough, he did so and taking careful aim, shot and killed him.

A lull in the fighting, gave Adams the chance to engage the SS officer in conversation. The German wasn't intractable and seemed prepared to discuss anything that the American brought up. He told his captor: 'Germany must and will, win the war. However, it must be over by the end of 1945 since they can't carry on the fight much longer than that. Germany is saving England and the rest of Europe from Russia. Why is the U.S.A. involved in a war which doesn't concern it?'

Lieutenant Adams replied, 'We Americans are fighting against such things as the atrocities committed by your soldiers on the eastern front.'

The German responded, 'Do you know the Russians?'

'Yes, they are our allies and good soldiers.'

'If you knew them, you wouldn't like them. We have new weapons to help us win the war.'

'What about the condition of Berlin?'

'The allied air raids have done much damage, but as fast as buildings are destroyed, we re-build them. Most of our factories are underground. We'll spend Christmas in Paris.'

Adams finished the conversation and re-joined his men at the windows. From there, he spotted enemy infantry running to and fro through a gap in a garden hedgerow. After watching this performance for a few minutes, he picked up his carbine, modified to make it fully automatic when desired. Resting the weapon on the stone windowsill, he pointed it at the gap in the hedge, past which he'd seen the enemy soldiers running. Every time a German appeared in the gap, he fired and by late afternoon, numerous German dead lay piled in the gap, victims of Adams' marksmanship. The Germans then stopped using the gap as an avenue of approach to wherever they'd been going. Throughout the afternoon, artillery fire, both American and German, never ceased as gunners pounded the villages from all sides. During the afternoon, Colonel Boos moved his 38th Infantry regimental command post from number 95 Rocherath, to a new location on the south side of Krinkelt.

At about 16:00, a German tank fired shells at the 2nd Platoon position and minutes later a second tank pulled up at the junction of the main street with the water tower road and fired a couple of rounds into the building. One round burst inside the house, destroying the stairs leading to the first floor. Amidst the choking smoke and dust, mingled with the stench of cordite, Lieutenant Adams ordered his men to vacate the building. Down in the basement, the civilians remained; unaware of the fact the Americans had left. Adams' men crouched in a ditch to the rear of the house, their visibility restricted by the clouds of billowing smoke which arose from the partially demolished Drösch family home. The terrified civilians could hear a wounded man screaming in the house above them. Maria Drösch cautiously crept up the steps to find a badly wounded SS man lying on her floor. At great personal risk, she dragged the wounded man to safety.

Some 1,000 yards south of Krinkelt, as they passed the sawmill, the lead elements of Captain McGee's column came under artillery fire. To the gunners of 2nd Division artillery, this draw was an ideal avenue of approach for German troops attacking Krinkelt. As the shells rained down, Sergeant Wilhelm of Company D, 393rd Infantry yelled 'Make a break for the bridge!' Crossing the small bridge, they came upon a small group of American trucks, in each of which, the driver sat dead at the wheel, his cab riddled with bullets. Among the vehicles, an ambulance full of wounded soldiers had been machine-gunned, killing both its crew and patients. Among the dead was Sergeant Elmer P. Klug of Company L, 394th who'd been evacuated from Buchholz two days previous with a broken neck. Sergeant Wilhelm and his men started walking up the road that was strewn with abandoned Christmas packages towards Krinkelt.

Sergeant Schaefer also took part in this incident at the saw mill and later wrote of his experiences there:

> *Once past the mill area, the artillery lifted and we continued along the creek until we reached the wrecked bridge on the Büllingen to Krinkelt road. Here we met the 2nd Division men who were still holding this portion of the road. Jerry had captured Büllingen but had been repulsed in his attempt to reach Krinkelt down this road.* [Author's note: In the action involving Lieutenant Owen R. McDermott of Company C, 644th Tank Destroyer Battalion and Lieutenant Carlo Biggio of Battery C, 372nd Field Artillery Battalion.] *With a sigh of relief, we entered friendly territory after three days behind enemy lines. We gave up our walking wounded to the medics and the rest of us continued onto Wirtzfeld then Elsenborn.*

Sergeant Bernard MacKay of Company B, 393rd Infantry, was wounded while passing through the draw, receiving shrapnel wounds to his back, right leg and right foot. The blast tore his left overshoe and combat boot off without injuring the foot. A friend of MacKay's, Leon Didier pulled MacKay and another wounded man to safety. A medic bandaged their wounds and did his best to make them both feel as comfortable as possible. Worn out by sixty hours of action and wandering around the forest, MacKay and the others sought refuge in an abandoned dugout and pulled empty ammunition boxes up to block the entrance.

Captain McGee's stragglers had contested every foot of the forest from their positions along the International Highway. The Germans had paid dearly for those few square miles of woodland and despite the alleged cowardice of his battalion commander, Captain McGee had managed to lead 570 officers and men back to the safety of US lines. Major Legler's 1st Battalion, 393rd Infantry came off worse, as only 300 of its effectives made it back to Krinkelt.

Since personally supervising the withdrawal of his division from the Wahlerscheid salient, General Robertson had kept a close eye on events in the Twin Villages. Brigadier General John H. Stokes Jr., the Deputy Commanding General of the 2nd Division had incorporated into combat some 2,000 men of the 99th Division. Among them was Colonel Mackenzie's 395th Regimental Combat Team, just east of the Wahlerscheid road, north of Baracken.

At 13:30 on the 18th, General Robertson held a conference with General Lauer and Major General Clift Andrus of the 1st Infantry Division. The three men agreed upon an accepted plan of action. At around 17:00, that same day, V Corps advised Robertson that the 99th Division was now under

TO CGS CLN SECOND AND NINENINE INS DIVS FROM CG FIFTH CORPS

//1816 A

NINENINE INF DIV ATTACHED TO SECOND INF DIV PD CG SECOND INF DIV

ASSUMES COMMAND EFFECTIVE ONEEIGHTONEEIGHTXEROXEROABLE DEC PD CG

NINENINE INF DIV WILL ACT AS DEPUTY COMMANDER TO THE CG SECOND

INF DIV

AUTHEN

Received in .... code

106. The document placing the 99th Infantry Division under the command of General Robertson with General Lauer acting as his deputy. (99th Division Archives)

his command and that General Lauer was to act as his deputy. By then, it was obvious that the Twin Villages were untenable, since both flanks were wide open to attack by the enemy. Furthermore, it was impossible to link the defenders of Krinkelt-Rocherath with the 9th Infantry Division just north of Elsenborn, or the 1st Infantry Division southwest of Wirtzfeld in Bütgenbach. General Robertson's mission of holding the Twin Villages until all 99th Division stragglers had passed through was now complete. The arrival in Krinkelt of Captain McGee's column meant that the way was now open for withdrawal to the Elsenborn Ridge. The majority of 99th troops likely to escape encirclement in the forest had done so. Over the next few days, only small groups and individuals would emerge to join the defenders on the high ground between Elsenborn and Berg.

In Rocherath, Lieutenant Adams and his men were still in the ditch to the rear of number 65. Adams went to find Captain Rollings who, despite a leg wound, was still on the go. Adams tried to secure permission to abandon the Drösch home but Captain Rollings reply was short and to the point: 'Hell no! Get back there; that is a key position.'

As soon as the dust had settled enough to allow them to breathe, the 2nd Platoon returned to the house. They re-established their defense of the building with their machine gun at a window and the riflemen as guards.

General Stokes had reason to be proud of his men, whose courage and tenacity had so far kept the Germans from capturing the Twin Villages. This tenacity was exemplified in a remark made by Colonel Norris of the 2nd Battalion, 38th Infantry. When an enemy tank pulled up outside his command post he yelled to his staff 'Bolt the windows! They're coming through the door.'

Just before dark, Lieutenant George W. Stewart, leader of the Anti-tank Company Mine Platoon, received an order telling him to report to the regimental command post. Colonel Norris told him that he wanted him to transport mines to each of the rifle companies in turn. Lieutenant Stewart got four enlisted men and two sergeants from the battalion to act as guides. On his first trip, Stewart and his men hand-carried fifty mines to Company E, passing through a house so as not to be seen by the enemy. One of the enlisted men remained with Company E. The next job was to get mines to Companies F and G, which were further away. Quickly, Stewart's men loaded 100 mines onto a jeep trailer. With two men riding the trailer, the jeep sped off into the night. About 500 yards from their destination, they came upon a German tank stood on the east side of the street. The jeep screeched to a halt as a heavily accented German voice called out in English for them to surrender.

The two men riding the trailer jumped into a roadside ditch and the driver put the vehicle in gear then roared off at top speed. Two Germans standing beside the tank fired their rifles at the fleeing vehicle. After their lucky escape, Lieutenant Stewart and his men (minus the two in the ditch) reached their destination and went to work laying mines.

A burning halftrack outside the Drösch home lit up the entire street. Since his platoon was split between two houses and because number 61 was impossible to defend at night due to a blind spot to the east, Lieutenant Adams pulled back his easternmost squad and used them to reinforce his own position. At the same time, US artillery opened fire in a target area that seemed to enclose Adams and his men in a semicircular wall of fire, interposed between them and the enemy. The fire continued all night long and the 2nd Platoon derived a great deal of comfort from it. Between 22:00 and 23:00, a group of four enemy tanks led by a German-manned Sherman, came past the Company C command post with their lights on. The Sherman deceived the Americans, who mistook the tanks for friendly armor. They hailed the tanks in English and, when there was no answer, opened fire on them. Unaffected, the four tanks moved away and were not seen again.

During the course of that day, another communications failure had occurred that could have had a disastrous effect upon the men involved. At about 02:00 on 18 December, General Robertson had radioed Colonel Mackenzie's 395th Regimental Combat Team to maintain contact with the 38th Infantry and, at the same time, prepare for the move to Elsenborn. At about 16:00, a radio message reached the 395th regimental command post ordering the regiment to begin withdrawal towards Elsenborn. Colonel Mackenzie's radio operator authenticated the message twice over the radio channel. Colonel Mackenzie set out in person for the division command post in order to verify the message. Prior to his departure, he left instructions that he would meet his 1st and 2nd battalions at a given point. Upon reaching the 99th Division command post at Dom Rurhof near Sourbrodt, General Lauer told him that no such message had been sent. Mackenzie immediately returned to meet his withdrawing units at the pre-arranged location. He ordered his battalion commanders to return to their original positions, but Major Alfred Stevens of the 2nd Battalion, refused to comply, so Mackenzie immediately relieved him of command. The battalion executive officer, Major Robert L. Boyden, replaced Stevens and led the men back to their original position, arriving there around 23:00.

Since the war, various theories have been advanced as to the origin of this radio message. It is possible, but unlikely, that the Germans had sent it using a captured US radio. Officers in the 99th Division intelligence section, believed that it was sent and either mixed up in transmission or at the receiving end. This was the only 'phony' message of the day, so it would seem that if the Germans had captured the code, they would have made more use of it. The *990th Regiment* of *277th Volksgrenadier Division* was in position just east of the 395th Regimental Combat Team and never reacted to the temporary withdrawal. They either failed to notice it or were reluctant to risk offensive action in the darkness.

By midnight, 18 December, General Robertson faced a different problem. He had to release Colonel Mackenzie's 395th Regimental Combat Team so that its men could return to Elsenborn for reorganization within their own division. The 2nd Division's withdrawal from the Twin Villages and the establishment of a cohesive defense atop the Elsenborn Ridge had to take place simultaneously.

The German failure to break through at Krinkelt-Rocherath on the 18th brought about a change in the tactics employed by the *1st* SS *Panzerkorps*. *Generaloberst* Dietrich suggested to *Generalleutnant* Herman Priess, that the *12th SS* disengage, swing southwest, bypass Bütgenbach and then get back on Rollbahn 'C', west of the American defenders. Priess disagreed, believing that the Twin Villages and Bütgenbach must be cleared in order to open a better road net. Eventually, the two men reached a compromise whereby late on the 18th, the *12th SS* began withdrawal from the Twin Villages sector and *Generalmajor* Walter Denkert's *3rd Panzergrenadier Division* moved in to take its place. *Oberstleutnant* Gerhard Lemcke's *89th Fusilier Regiment* of the *12th Volksgrenadier Division* kept up its attacks towards Krinkelt from the direction of Mürringen. *Brigadeführer* Hugo Kraas was to disengage his *Hitlerjugend* as quickly as possible and join a combat team of the *12th Volksgrenadier Division* in an attack against the US flank position at Bütgenbach. This transfer of armor and its subsequent replacement by mechanized infantry would mean that future attacks against the Twin Villages would lack the momentum required to make any significant penetration of the American line.

Chapter Fourteen

Krinkelt –Rocherath

19 December 1944

In the early morning light of 19 December, and under cover of a dense fog, German infantrymen resumed their attacks against the villages. The Americans met all such attacks with a heavy defensive barrage, courtesy of the 2nd, 9th, 99th and V Corps artillery battalions positioned on Elsenborn Ridge.

Once again, Colonel Boos' 38th Infantry prepared to do battle for this important yet small patch of Belgium. At 08:00, having spent the night in a house in the Company G position, Lieutenant George W. Stewart decided to rejoin his own platoon. He collected his three men and they loaded several wounded men onto their jeep trailer, then heading up the main street, passed the spot occupied by the enemy tank the previous evening, but it had gone. Arriving at his platoon command post, Lieutenant Stewart discovered, much to his relief, that the two men who had jumped off the trailer, the previous night, had returned safe and well.

107. A Panther tank of 12th SS knocked out on main street, Rocherath. (Courtesy Tom C. Morris)

108. One of the Panthers and the assault gun knocked out by Captain James W. Love and Private Isabel Salazar of Anti-tank Company 38th Infantry just west of the water tower in Rocherath. (Courtesy Tom C. Morris)

109. Two of the Panthers knocked out in Rocherath. (Courtesy Paul Drösch)

110. *Panthers knocked out in front of the Kalpers house on main street, Rocherath. (Tom C. Morris)*

111. *The two Panthers and assault gun knocked out just west of the water tower in Rocherath. (Courtesy Tom C. Morris)*

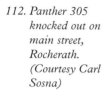

112. *Panther 305 knocked out on main street, Rocherath. (Courtesy Carl Sosna)*

113. *The assault gun and Panthers knocked out just west of the water tower in Rocherath by Captain James W. Love and Private Isabel Salazar of Anti-tank Company 38th Infantry.*

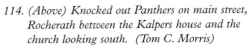

114. *(Above) Knocked out Panthers on main street, Rocherath between the Kalpers house and the church looking south. (Tom C. Morris)*

115. *(Left) Panther 305 on main street, Rocherath. (Courtesy Glen Kieffer/Bill Warnock)*

116. *(Below) A view of the church after the battle. (Courtesy Ed Jordan)*

117. Panther 305 on main street,
*   Rocherath. (Courtesy Glen Kieffer/*
*   Bill Warnock)*

At 09:00, a platoon of German
infantry moved into number 61
Rocherath, abandoned, the night
before by Lieutenant Adams' 2nd
Squad. Captain Edward Rollings,
commanding Company C, ordered
a US tank destroyer to fire three
rounds into the building. The
Germans could be seen carrying
wounded out of number 61 for
forty-five minutes after the tank
destroyer fired. As the evacuation
of German wounded progressed,
an enemy tank, accompanied by
infantry, appeared across the street
from Captain Rollings' command
post. Company C opened fire with

118. A view of Krinkelt taken from the church steeple after the battle.
*   (Cavanagh collection origin unknown)*

every weapon they had, and the tank returned fire. Captain Rollings yelled for Lieutenant Adams to grab a bazooka and finish off the tank. Adams grabbed a bazooka, and climbed into what was left of the attic of number 65, where Sergeant Rudolf Kraft, also carrying a bazooka, joined him. The two men decided to fire in unison at the tank and on the count of three did so. Unfortunately, Adams' weapon failed to function. But Sergeant Kraft's projectile hit the tank's bogie wheels. Discarding his useless weapon, Adams took over as loader for Kraft. A second rocket penetrated the tank turret and burst inside. As Adams bent forward to load a third rocket for his sergeant, a high velocity tank round tore into the attic, exploded and piled debris from the wall and ceiling over the two Americans. A second shell entered the attic and burst harmlessly against the far wall. Adams and Kraft sprang to their feet and rushed downstairs to the basement as the enemy tank continued firing. By then, the Belgian civilians in the cellar were convinced that they were about to die. In between shots fired by the tank, Adams' men ran to the windows on the ground floor to return fire. This duel lasted till about noon, when a further two enemy tanks showed up at the junction with the water tower road. One of these tanks fired a couple of shells into the Drösch home, and then set a nearby wooden barn alight with its machine gun.

119. The Drösch house being rebuilt after the battle. A knocked out Panther can be made out to the rear and in front of house number 64 in the background. (Courtesy Paul Drösch)

120. *Lieutenant George Adams and the men of his 2nd Platoon, Company C of the 38th Infantry defended the Drösch house, pictured before the battle. (Courtesy Paul Drösch)*

Adams went to the company command post to give Captain Rollings a report on his situation. He had been injured when the attic wall collapsed on top of him and needed medical attention. Attempts to evacuate him by jeep failed, so he decided to leave on foot. Amidst the smoke, gunfire and the battle noise, George W. Adams turned his back on the Drösch home, for which he'd developed a kind of affinity, and set off for the nearest aid station. Another officer from Company C, Lieutenant Roy E. Mode, tried to extinguish the fire in the woodshed, but wasn't able to do so. Soon the flames spread to the house and a GI ran down the basement steps to warn the civilians. Opening the cellar door, the man shouted 'Home brennt; you must go!'

Snatching what meager possessions they could, the battle weary villagers followed the American out of the burning building. Under covering small-arms fire they ran, heads down, along a track past number 64, the Melchior house, in the direction of Wirtzfeld. Upon reaching Wirtzfeld, the hapless civilians were evacuated to Verviers, Belgium by truck. They had escaped from the very bowels of hell and behind them, in Rocherath, smoke and flames engulfed the Drösch home.

In Elsenborn, Captain Robert W. Bricker of Battery A, 535th Anti-aircraft Automatic Weapons Battalion, and ten of his men, all volunteers, set out back towards burning Krinkelt in an attempt to recover their abandoned halftracks. The vehicles had got themselves stuck in the mud northwest of Krinkelt on the night of 17 December. Bricker's men winched, towed, and drove several halftracks, Bofors guns, two and a half ton trucks, and a few jeeps to Elsenborn. Captain Bricker fulfilled a promise he'd made to himself on the 17th, when he swore to return and retrieve the lost vehicles. Captain Bricker earned himself a Silver Star for his role in evacuating the guns and vehicles.

General Stokes was by now ready to evacuate the Twin Villages. Colonel Boos ordered his men to quietly destroy all German and American equipment, which couldn't be brought out. At 13:45, General Stokes gave the withdrawal order to take effect from 17:30 hours. Colonel Mackenzie's 395th Regimental Combat Team was to retire across country along a single boggy trail to Elsenborn. This small trail would later become the main German supply route in their attacks against the Elsenborn Ridge.

The 38th Infantry and attached troops, who were more closely engaged, were to break away from the villages, fall back through Wirtzfeld, then move along the makeshift road between Berg and Elsenborn, which had been constructed by the 2nd Engineer Combat Battalion. The 38th was to occupy a new defensive position west and northwest of Wirtzfeld. Once the regiment was in position, the units occupying Wirtzfeld were to withdraw.

Regiment briefed the company commanders and urged them not to mention the word 'withdrawal' in instructions to their men. Instead, they would refer to 'A move to new positions'. The move would be orderly and the men were to 'walk not run'. A rearguard was to lay mines and beat off any pursuing enemy. It would comprise engineers, elements of the 741st Tank Battalion and the 3rd Platoon of Company C, 644th Tank Destroyer Battalion.

Disengagement from the action in the Twin Villages was made from left to right along the line from Rocherath to Wirtzfeld. Colonel Norris pulled his 2nd Battalion, 38th Infantry back first from the northern end of Rocherath, and Colonel Mildren's 1st Battalion followed. At the junction in Krinkelt leading west to Wirtzfeld, Colonel Barsanti assumed command of a small composite rearguard. As the Germans moved into Rocherath, Private Truman Kimbro of Company C, 2nd Engineer Combat Battalion, was a member of a squad ordered to block a road in the village. In trying to reach his objective, he found it occupied by an enemy tank and about twenty infantrymen. Kimbro ignored the danger and, carrying mines, he braved enemy fire in his attempt to block the road. As he made his way forward alone, he drew heavy enemy fire, which badly wounded him. He nonetheless continued and dragged himself into position so as to lay the mines. His mission complete, he tried to return to his squad but was cut to pieces by enemy rifle and machine-

121. *Captain Harlow F. Lennon, Lieutenant Charles Coats and Lieutenant Bob Grant of Company C, 644th Tank Destroyer Battalion.*
(Courtesy Paul Stevenson)

gun fire. Kimbro's bravery earned him a posthumous Medal of Honor. As the last engineer platoon passed through his position, Colonel Barsanti was convinced that he and his men would manage to leave Krinkelt alive. Barsanti's men placed a 'daisy chain' of mines across the road, and then they and the engineers jumped aboard two M-10 tank destroyers that roared off in the direction of Wirtzfeld.

Lieutenant Charlie Coats, who had just returned from leave on a three-day pass to Verviers, commanded these tank destroyers. Coats had returned to Krinkelt on the 19th to reassume command of the 3rd Platoon of Company C, 644th Tank Destroyer Battalion. Just east of the village, they crossed a small temporary bridge over the Wirtzbach creek and one of the engineers asked Lieutenant Coats to stop so they could destroy the bridge. The job done, they continued to Wirtzfeld, then occupied by elements of the 9th Infantry Regiment. The tank destroyers made their way to a temporary bivouac area in the vicinity of Bütgenbach where determined soldiers of the 1st Infantry Division were busy digging in. At 02:00, on 20 December, a rearguard tank platoon of the 741st Tank Battalion left Wirtzfeld, closely followed by the foot troops of the 9th Infantry. One thousand yards west of Wirtzfeld these infantrymen passed through the newly established 38th Infantry defense line.

The battle for Krinkelt-Rocherath was over, having cost both sides dearly in men and *matériel*. The outcome favored the Americans, by then firmly entrenched atop the Elsenborn Ridge. All future enemy attacks against the ridge positions would lack the element of surprise as well as the tank and artillery support that had enabled the Germans to reach the Twin Villages.

The 99th Infantry Division had received its 'Baptism of fire' under circumstances that were quite arduous in terms of combat in the western European theater. More than ninety per cent of the division's losses were suffered during the period 16-19 December. In four days, the 99th had lost fourteen officers and 119 men killed in action. Some fifty-three officers and 1,341 men were missing in action and further fifty-one officers and 864 men were listed as wounded in action. The 99th Division clearing station processed about 600 non-battle casualties before 20 December, half of which were trench foot cases before that date. Among the missing were Sergeant MacKay of Company B, 393rd Infantry, his two friends Leon Didier and Bruce Harrison and the two medics who'd joined them. They remained in their dugout on the outskirts of Krinkelt, throughout 19 December. They had jammed an ammunition box up against the entrance in order to keep out the cold. Realizing that all friendly troops had left the vicinity, they decided to wait in the hope of a possible American counter-attack.

Through the gaps between the logs that formed the dugout, they had a good all round view and during the night of 19 December, one of the non-wounded men went out in search of food. The following morning, they heard the sound of someone rummaging around outside and through the gaps they spotted a German soldier filling a canvas bag with booty. Now and then, he would discard an object when he found something more interesting. Despite their predicament, the Americans found the situation to be quite humorous. Leon Didier wanted to shoot the enemy soldier, but Sergeant MacKay ordered him not to do so. MacKay hoped that the German might overlook the dugout and believed that the sound of a shot might only serve to attract other Germans.

Approaching the dugout, his MP-40 machine pistol at the ready, the German kicked aside the ammunition box and shouted for the Americans to give themselves up. MacKay and Harrison couldn't walk so the German ordered the others to start a nearby jeep. They refused for fear that the vehicle might be booby-trapped, so their captor decided to let them walk into Krinkelt as best they could. The non-wounded helped MacKay and Harrison as the German walked about fifteen yards behind his prisoners. As they entered the village, they couldn't help but notice numerous bodies, American and German, frozen in the most grotesque positions. Once in Krinkelt, the German took them to a house near the church where an officer questioned them but learned nothing of value. He drew a pistol and put it to Sergeant Macay's head, asking further fruitless questions. By that time, MacKay felt terrible and didn't much care whether he died or not. The German pulled the trigger and the firing pin struck an empty chamber with a sharp click. The enemy officer and three men with him burst into laughter as he patted MacKay on the shoulder and told him 'You and your friends are good soldiers!'

He then sent for a German aid man who examined and treated their wounds. The following day, Didier and the American medics left on a long trek into captivity. The Germans placed MacKay and Harrison inside an ambulance full of their own wounded and drove them to an aid station packed with wounded Germans. Following further examination, MacKay and Harrison also ended up in a German POW camp.

General Robertson's 2nd Infantry Division had likewise suffered numerous casualties. Since the 2nd Division began its action in this sector during the attack on Wahlerscheid, it is not possible to determine the ratio between casualties suffered in the first three days of the attack on Wahlerscheid and during the subsequent defense of the Twin Villages. No concrete total is available for the period 13-19 December 1944.

The 9th Infantry saw action both at Wahlerscheid and in the Twin Villages. It listed forty-seven officers and men as killed in action, 425 as being wounded and 192 were listed as missing in action. A further 600 men

122. The church as
seen from the road
to Büllingen.
(Courtesy Ed
Jordan)
Inset 123: A view of
the church from the
south after the battle.
(Courtesy Tom C
Morris)

124. (Above) The damaged church steeple after the 2nd Division recaptured the Twin Villages. (Courtesy Tom. C. Morris)

125. (Left) The church shortly before demolition. (Author's collection, origin unknown)

126. (Right) Wrecked vehicles in front of the church. (Courtesy Tom C. Morris)

127. *Wrecked vehicles in front of the church.* (Author's collection)

128. *A tank of the 741st Tank Battalion knocked out by the side of the church.*
(Author's collection, courtesy Tom C. Morris)

129. (Right) The interior of the church. (Author's collection, origin unknown)

130. (Below) A soldier of the 2nd Division ponders the state of the church interior. (US Army photograph)

131. (Above) The church entrance after the battle. (Courtesy Carl Sosna)

132. (Left) The church after the battle. (Courtesy Carl Sosna)

were listed as non-battle casualties. Losses due to respiratory diseases and trench foot were particularly high. The ferocity of the battle to occupy and then defend the Twin Villages after the Wahlerscheid attack is visible in the battle losses suffered by the 38th Infantry. Some 389 officers and men were reported as missing in action (many had been killed but not so counted, since the Americans subsequently gave up the area). Fifty men were wounded and evacuated; the list of those killed in action underestimated the number at eleven. All told, the 38th Infantry suffered 625 casualties in its three days at Krinkelt-Rocherath. Precise

133. *The Panther knocked out by Lieutenant Robert A. Parker and Private John G. Cullinane of Reconnaissance Company 644th Tank Destroyer Battalion. (Courtesy Tom C. Morris)*

134. *Panthers knocked out in front of the Kalpers house on main street, Rocherath. (Courtesy Tom C Morris)*

135. GIs discussing the merits of the Panther. (Courtesy Tom C. Morris)

136. Panthers in front of the Kalpers house on main street, Rocherath. (Courtesy Tom C Morris)

figures for the losses suffered by the 23rd Infantry Regiment are not available but are thought to equal those of the other two regiments of the division.

The successful defense of the Twin Villages can be attributed to the teamwork and sheer tenacity displayed by General Robertson, his men and those of the supporting tank destroyer and tank battalions. Initially, the infantry secured and held the ground. Subsequently, they called upon artillery, tank and tank destroyer support, in their defense of the villages. The effectiveness of artillery support cannot be over emphasized. In his battalion's defense of the Lausdell crossroads, Colonel McKinley relied heavily upon artillery to stop German armor in its tracks. He later stated:

It was the artillery that did the job. On three different occasions, artillery support, when and where it was vitally needed, saved my battalion from decimation and the last time from complete destruction.

During the period 17–19 December, 2nd Division gunners fired thous-ands of rounds non-stop. German troops soon learned to fear the deadly TOT (Time on Target) barrages fired by US artillery. The 2nd

137. *The Panthers knocked out in front of the Kalpers house on main street, Rocherath. (Courtesy Tom C. Morris)*

Division and its organic artillery battalions perfected their own firing procedures for a TOT mission. In the divisional operations section they installed a push button box with five buttons, one for each organic battalion and a fifth for an attached battalion. These buttons were connected to each battalion by ground-return circuit and didn't pass through a switchboard. The touch of a button would result in an instantaneous ring in one or all battalion operations sections. When a TOT was to be fired, Division Artillery would call each battalion individually to give coordinates, nature of the target, method of fire and ask them to call back when ready. When the last battalion had done so, the fire direction center sent out a warning signal consisting of three buzzes. They did so by pushing all buttons simultaneously. Fifteen seconds later, after one long buzz, the operations officer would start his stopwatch. Exactly one minute after this last buzz, all rounds fired were expected to burst over the target. The proficiency with which 2nd Division Artillery delivered such devastating fire both impressed and terrified the enemy. One result of the intense involvement of US artillery in the battle was the high casualty rate among its forward observers.

Captain Harlow F. Lennon's Company C, 644th Tank Destroyer Battalion, and the attached 2nd Platoon of Company A under 2nd Lieutenant Phil Di Carlo, had performed admirably in and around the Twin Villages. The unit's tank destroyers knocked out twenty-three pieces of enemy armor, while First Lieutenant Robert Parker of the battalion Reconnaissance Company and a jeep driver, Private John Cullinane, knocked out two more using a bazooka they borrowed from nearby infantry.

The 801st Tank Destroyer Battalion was mainly composed of towed guns and suffered losses in equipment as a result. Between 17 and 19 December, the unit lost seventeen guns and sixteen halftracks. Its 3-inch guns were in position alongside the infantry and were thus exposed to intense enemy shelling. Furthermore these guns could not be moved at night. The battalion's halftracks carried an ample supply of mines that were put to good use by adjacent riflemen. Many of the unit's gun crews served valiantly as infantry, once their guns had been destroyed. Nonetheless, there were instances when the towed guns proved lethal to the enemy. Near Hünningen, one such gun had knocked out four enemy tanks before being put out of action itself.

The 741st Tank Battalion, supporting the 2nd Division, was a tried and tested unit that lost numerous duplex drive tanks off Omaha Beach on D-Day. In its fierce three-day encounter with the Germans in Krinkelt-Rocherath, the 741st tankers showed themselves to be adept in the art of waylaying and killing an assortment of enemy armor. Their Sherman tanks were no match for the heavier German armor in a head on confrontation, so they compensated for this by setting up ambush type situations throughout the villages.

From well-camouflaged positions with expert manoeuvering and stalking, the battalion's gunners destroyed twenty-seven tanks, one self-propelled gun, two armored cars, two halftracks and two trucks. In contrast, the battalion lost eight tanks to enemy action. Another two got bogged down, so the crews destroyed them while a third, of which the engine was 'scuttled', was abandoned.

Among the infantry anti-tank weapons used was the 57mm anti-tank gun. Supposedly a mobile piece, it proved useless in the Ardennes mud. A highly vulnerable weapon, its shells often bounced off the heavy frontal armor of German tanks. One well-placed shot could wreck the gun and kill its crew and by the end of the battle, both the 2nd and 99th Divisions recommended the abolition of the 57mm gun as an infantry anti-tank weapon.

During their withdrawal from Wahlerscheid, the rifle battalions had either left their mines in the forest or with the battalion transport. The numerous stragglers and US vehicular columns passing along the same routes as oncoming enemy armor made the use of mines too risky. At the Lausdell crossroads, Colonel McKinley's 1st Battalion, 9th Infantry, did tie mines together in order to pull them across the road in front of oncoming tanks. The 3.2 inch bazooka proved to be a highly valuable weapon in the hands of infantrymen who used the cover provided by hedgerows, walls and buildings to stalk their prey. In their stubborn defense of the Twin Villages, American soldiers had destroyed at least 111 enemy tanks, assault guns and armored vehicles.

138. Lieutenant Robert A. Parker of Reconnaissance Company, 644th Tank Destroyer Battalion who earned a DSC in Krinkelt. (Courtesy Robert A. Parker)

On 19 December, officers of the German General Staff appeared in the area, their mission to find out why their combat commanders had failed to achieve a complete breakthrough. It seemed, in their opinion, that two main factors had led to their troops being stalled in the sector. Naturally, they chose to officially ignore the existence of tough resistance by the US defenders. Instead, they chose to lay the blame for failure upon poor roads and inadequate training of troops committed to the attack. It was a fact that the area road net provided a somewhat restricted avenue of approach to the west. A major headache faced by the 'on the spot' German commanders were the ubiquitous traffic jams. Poor training of troops was also partially to blame, especially in the case of the *277th Volksgrenadier Division*, its ranks filled with redundant sailors and airmen. Inexperience on the German side was offset by a similar state of affairs in the 99th Division. The Germans enjoyed numerical superiority, which was boosted by the near absence of Allied air power. The visiting German General Staff officers reached the following conclusion:

> *In order for the attack to regain its momentum, the right wing of 6th Panzer Army had to be brought abreast of the 1st SS whose lead unit had reached a point two miles west of Stoumont. Since the Elsenborn Ridge dominated the area, it now had to be taken. In moving the 'Hitlerjugend' out of Krinkelt-Rocherath to attack Dom Bütgenbach, the Germans hoped to move west on the Büllingen-Malmedy highway.*

Chapter Fifteen

The 'Big Red One'
at Dom Bütgenbach

18-22 December 1944

In Bütgenbach, troops of the 26th Infantry Regiment, 1st Infantry Division, covered the 2nd Division flank and rear. The area between Bütgenbach and Wirtzfeld was not suited to enemy offensive operations since it consisted of a large lake, the Bütgenbachersee, and a multitude of small streams. Consolidation of US defensive positions atop Elsenborn Ridge meant that the Germans had to capture the road to Bütgenbach.

In order to best defend the road, Lieutenant Colonel Daniel's 2nd Battalion, 26th Infantry, occupied the high ground and a cluster of farm buildings at Dom Bütgenbach. Colonel Daniel emphasized the need to hold the position at all costs. The 2nd Platoon of the 26th Infantry Regimental Anti-tank Company, Company C of the 634th Tank Destroyer Battalion and the 2nd Platoon of Company C, 745th Tank Battalion were attached in support of Daniel's men.

The 26th Infantry Regiment held an unfavorable position as it was separated from the rest of the division. This was nothing new to the men of the 1st Infantry Division, many of whom had seen service in North Africa, Sicily and Normandy. Despite the fact that the lake protected the 26th Infantry's left flank, the 2nd Battalion position jutted out beyond this cover. The regimental right flank was also exposed there, as the 26th Infantry was theoretically responsible for the defense of four miles of terrain between Bütgenbach and Waimes.

The 2nd Battalion position offered little concealment as the area was almost totally devoid of cover. The unit took over the large stone manor house for it to serve as both command post and aid station. The walls were quite thick and offered adequate cover against enemy artillery and mortar fire. The third floor offered good observation over the entire battalion position and Colonel Daniel's men made an effort to camouflage the position so as to reduce the effectiveness of enemy observation. The unit was at eighty per cent full strength and of its men, about sixty per cent of whom were replacements. It had recently suffered heavy losses in its fight to clear part of the Hurtgen Forest. At the suggestion of his operations officer,

Colonel Daniel adopted the motto 'We fight and die here' for his unit's defense of Dom Bütgenbach.

In anticipation of heavy enemy artillery and mortar fire, Colonel Daniel ordered that all his riflemen and front line crew carrying weapons be provided with overhead log cover. Wire teams laid three communications lines to each company and made sure that no two lines were laid over the same route. Radio and messenger communication supplemented wire. Both 60 and 81mm mortar ammunition was stacked by the weapons as battalion expected heavy enemy attacks.

During the night of 18-19 December, the *1st SS Panzerkorps* prepared its attack. The *12th SS* moved its forward command post to Büllingen to direct this attack. The division's armor made its way to the village via Losheimergraben along Rollbahn 'C', by then a quagmire, and upon arrival in Büllingen SS officers reported that the tanks on the route were churned into the mud to a depth of four feet.

At 02:15 on 19 December, the enemy launched his first major thrust towards Dom Bütgenbach. Some twenty truckloads of *SS Panzergrenadiers* dismounted from their trucks just west of Büllingen then deployed behind a dozen tanks to move against the 2nd Battalion position on the high ground. Company F called for artillery support and the 33rd Field Artillery Battalion fired 105mm howitzer fire, white phosphorous and illuminating shells down upon the attackers. Some of the German tanks got themselves bogged down prior to reaching the US lines; American bazooka teams and anti-tank gunners discouraged the rest. The 155mm guns of Colonel Rex Rowie's 5th Field Artillery Battalion lobbed high explosive shells on the remaining tanks and within an hour the attack petered out. At daylight, two patrols from Company F counted 100 enemy dead, three knocked out tanks and four destroyed trucks in front of their position.

Shortly after daylight broke, enemy artillery and mortar fire began falling on the positions and increased in intensity until 10:00. Ten minutes later, the Germans began probing attacks aimed at discovering weak points in the 2nd Battalion's 1,800 yard front. A company of *SS Panzergrenadiers*, supported by two tanks, attacked along the road from Morscheck. Colonel Daniel's men let them get within 100 yards of the company G position then opened fire with their 57mm anti-tank guns. Three rapid shots in quick succession knocked out both tanks although the lead tank did manage to get off one round, knocking out one of the anti-tank guns and killing two of the crew. Mortar and artillery fire wiped out the accompanying infantry. A few of those not killed managed to escape to the cover of a small wood only to be shot or taken prisoner by men of the Company E security post. The Germans postponed their next attack until enough men and tanks could be assembled in Büllingen.

During the night of 19-20 December, the German forces in Büllingen completed their assembly. At about 06:00, after an intense mortar and artillery barrage, twenty German tanks and a rifle battalion converged on Dom Bütgenbach from the south and east through the early morning fog. Since it was still dark, the 2nd Battalion mortar crews fired flares over the roads leading into the position. Heavy concentrations of US artillery put a stop to the advance by enemy infantry.

140. *The 12th SS Jagdpanzers knocked out in the dip to the west side of Büllingen. (Courtesy James W. Love)*

Staff Sergeant Stanley Odenski of the 1st Anti-tank Gun Squad, observed two tanks approaching his position. He sent a bazooka team to his right flank and took over the position of assistant anti-tank gunner on the 57mm gun himself. Sergeant Odenski ordered Corporal Henry F. Warner, a gunner, to commence firing. The tanks opened fire upon Colonel Daniel's command post, flames spurting from their gun barrels. Corporal Warner hit the nearest tank with four shots, knocking it out and setting it alight. Sergeant Odenski re-loaded and Warner knocked out a second tank with a further four well placed rounds. With the last shot, his gun's breechblock failed to close and the gun would not return to battery. A third tank appeared from the right and opened fire with its machine gun. Henry Warner's crew leapt into foxholes to seek cover, but Warner remained at his gun. The tank then attempted to run over the gun emplacement, but about ten feet from the gun, it stopped as the commander stuck his head and shoulders out of the hatch to direct the tank's movements. Warner drew a pistol and fired at the German, then jumped into his gun pit. The tank began moving away, its commander slumped dead over the edge of his turret. Having lost their commander, the crew seemed to have lost interest in any further combat. Intense US fire from tanks, tank destroyers and artillery broke up the enemy attack and the rest of the enemy force withdrew. Colonel Daniel's men stopped further minor attacks later in the day.

During the night of 20-21 December, engineers laid anti-tank mines along the 2nd Battalion's main line of resistance. Early on the morning of 21 December, the entire *26th SS Panzergrenadier Regiment*, plus elements of the *Panzer Regiment* prepared to attack Dom Bütgenbach. At 03:00, the Germans laid down an intense barrage of artillery mortar, tank and *Nebelwerfer* fire on the 2nd Battalion command post area. Heavy casualties resulted from direct hits scored upon foxholes and weapon emplacements. Initially, the Germans began to cross the fields in assault formation and American forward observers called on the support of ten field artillery battalions. Earlier, Colonel Daniel had taken the precaution of plotting likely enemy assembly areas and avenues of approach. A series of pre-arranged concentration numbers enabled supporting artillery to commence firing immediately. These artillerymen placed a 'ring of steel' around the 2nd Battalion, which proved most effective in breaking up the enemy infantry/tank formations. Some tanks and assault guns did get through only to be taken under fire by the remaining 57mm anti-tank guns. On the extreme right of the battalion's main line of resistance, facing due south was the Anti-tank Company gun squad commanded by Sergeant Noah Collier. This squad was protected by dense woods on its right flank and to its rear by two tanks and two M-10 tank destroyers. A BAR team protected Collier's gun emplacement against enemy infiltrating from the nearby woods.

When the shelling stopped, Sergeant Collier discovered that both members of the BAR team were wounded, so he arranged their evacuation. He then took over the BAR himself, ordering Corporal Irwin Schwartz to man the anti-tank gun. Collier poured fire into enemy infantry coming towards him from the woods. A German tank then moved forward and Private Donald Rose dropped his carbine to assist Schwartz on the anti-tank gun. He loaded a round of Sabot (a high velocity 57mm British shell) as Schwartz sighted then fired. The first shot hit the front left drive sprocket causing the tank to veer to the right and a second shot set the tank on fire.

Corporal Schwartz busied himself firing his carbine at enemy infantry then, as another enemy tank began its approach, he again manned the anti-tank gun. He scored three direct hits that put the vehicle out of action. No further tanks appeared, although the enemy infantry continued their attacks.

Schwartz and Rose grabbed their rifles and ran to Sergeant Collier who had sustained a leg wound. Despite his injury Collier maintained a deadly hail of fire against the advancing German infantry. As Schwartz and Rose reached him, an enemy *Panzerschreck* round hit the anti-tank gun, knocking it out of action and stunning the crew. Seconds later, the gun crew rejoined the fray and continued fighting until their ammunition ran out. They then withdrew through the heavy woods to the west in order to try and get more ammunition.

Some 200 yards to the left of Collier's gun, another crew, commanded by Staff Sergeant Kolar, opened fire on a new group of tanks. Machine-gun fire from the lead tank damaged Kolar's gun, so the sergeant grabbed a bazooka and set out to stalk the steel monster on foot. To his left, Corporal Joe Harris knocked out an enemy 150mm self propelled gun. Seconds later, a German tank put Harris' gun out of action.

To the east, some fifty yards from the main road leading south to St Vith, Corporal Henry Warner was manning his anti-tank gun single-handed, since his assistant gunner had been wounded. With his first shot, he hit the rear of an enemy tank that swung its turret around to meet him. As Henry Warner reloaded his gun, the tank's machine gun opened fire and with the shell half way in the chamber, Warner fell mortally wounded. He died trying in vain, to close the breech of the anti-tank gun. The battle for Dom Bütgenbach raged throughout the day with the 2nd Battalion not yielding an inch.

Thanks to continuous and effective artillery fire, for over eight hours, the Americans fired more than 10,000 rounds holding the Germans at bay. A group of nine German tanks managed to penetrate the main line of resistance, but for reasons unknown, six of them returned from whence they came. The remaining three tanks positioned themselves about seventy-five yards from Colonel Daniel's command post. From there, they opened fire on the building, using cannon and heavy machine guns. Colonel Daniel and his staff remained in the building and sought shelter in the basement. The adjoining room was filled with wounded men. Colonel Daniel kept in constant contact with the artillery fire direction center, making repeated requests for artillery support. Five SS men managed to get within ten yards of the command post but BAR fire mercilessly cut them down.

Four 90mm tank destroyers of the 613th Tank Destroyer Battalion arrived from Bütgenbach under cover of smoke. They took the enemy tanks under fire, destroying the first as it attempted to withdraw. They then destroyed the second tank, but the third made good its escape under cover of the smoke given off by one of the other two. By late afternoon, attacks by German infantry began to lose their momentum. Later that evening, a 2nd Battalion patrol probed the woods south of Dom Bütgenbach and counted over 300 dead enemy infantrymen.

The 2nd Battalion had suffered tremendous losses, but on the evening of 21 December, reinforcements arrived in the shape of Company C, of the 1st Division organic engineer battalion. The engineers quickly laid mines in front of the position. Several 4.2 inch mortars of the 2nd Division were also temporarily attached to the 2nd Battalion.

Just after daybreak, on 22 December, enemy patrols of the *26th SS Panzergrenadier Regiment*, 12th *SS Panzer Division* began to probe the 2nd Battalion lines. Just after 10:00, they attacked with a change in tactics. In place of a frontal assault, they attacked the battalion flanks and broke through on the right. Once more, US tank destroyers of the 613th Tank Destroyer Battalion stopped these attacks. By the day's end, the Germans were no nearer to capturing the road they so badly needed. The defenders of Dom Bütgenbach had lost four 57mm anti-tank guns and two tanks, compared with enemy losses of forty-seven armored vehicles and one self-propelled gun. Colonel Daniel's men held Dom Bütgenbach until 15 January 1945, when they resumed the offensive.

By 20 December, the Americans had completed a continuous line of defense on the Elsenborn Ridge. The 9th Infantry Division had moved into the Monschau-Kalterherberg sector, thus forming the northern flank of this defense line. By Christmas Day, the US line in the north was virtually unbroken. German attacks continued, but to no avail. On the Elsenborn Ridge the American GI shared the same freezing conditions and hardships as his German counterpart. The remnants of *12th SS Panzer Division* found themselves ordered to move south in order to support elements of *5th Panzer Army*.

The true grit shown by the soldiers of the 1st, 2nd and 99th Divisions in this northern sector was paramount in stopping the German advance. It first appeared at Wahlerscheid and along the International Highway, came to the fore at Lausdell and the Twin Villages, and then became apparent at Dom Bütgenbach and on the Elsenborn Ridge.

Today, the visitor to the sleepy, modern villages of Krinkelt-Rocherath can be forgiven for not realizing what happened there sixty years ago. With the passage of time, most of the scars have healed. A new church replaced that badly damaged during the battle and post war prosperity has enabled the people of the Twin Villages to resume normal lives.

Here and there, traces of the battle can still be found. Some of the

141. (Top Left) Men of the 741st Tank Battalion back in Krinkelt surveying the damage after the battle. (Courtesy Leonard Trimpe)

142. (Left) Soldiers of the 38th Infantry re-enter their former command post, the Faymonville house in Rocherath, after they recapture the Twin Villages. (Courtesy Tom C. Morris)

143. (Inset) An abandoned German truck on main street, Rocherath after the battle. (Tom C. Morris)

144. (Bottom) A GI looks over a German soldier killed in the Twin Villages after the Americans recaptured the area. (US Army photograph)

145. *The outskirts of Krinkelt after the battle. (Courtesy Tom C. Morris)*

146. *An SS man pinned beneath the tracks of a Panther knocked out in the Twin Villages. (Tom C. Morris)*

147. (Left) This house is the present a 'Vier Jahreszesten' restaurant with the road to the water tower off to the right. This photo was taken after the battle. (Courtesy Kendall M. Ogilvie)

148. (Below) Another view of the damage caused when a V-1 flying bomb hit a barn just east of house number 80, in Rocherath. (Courtesy Kendall M. Ogilvie)

149. (Below) This house, Number 80, Rocherath (still standing at the time of writing) served as the command post of Battery A of the 17 Field Artillery Observation Battalion. It is on the east side of the main street, just south of the junction leading east to the water tower. (Courtesy Kendall M. Ogilvie)

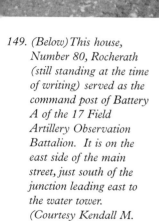

150. A view of the Kalpers house from the north. (Courtesy Bill Warnock/Glen Kieffer)

151. (Left) The same house as is shown on the left of picture 34 (Chapter 4, Page 50). This shot was taken after the battle. (Courtesy Kendall M. Ogilvie)

152. (Above) A painting by US Army artist Harrison Standley. It shows the junction with the main street and the road to the water tower after the battle. (US Army photograph)

153. (Right) A soldier of the 741st Tank Battalion sweeps the main street of the Twin Villages of mines after the battle. (Courtesy Leonard Trimpe)

civilians trapped in the Drösch home still live in the village, although number 65 had to be re-built, as did the Faymonville house that served as Colonel Boos' command post. Opposite the church, in a small park, two stone monuments commemorate the roll of the 2nd and 99th Divisions in the liberation of Belgium. A villager readily shows visitors an ornate leather pocket book recovered from the ruins of his parental home. It contains two photographs of people he presumes to be the parents of an American soldier. Some day, the man hopes to return the photos and the pocketbook to that soldier or his family.

In the forest, fast disappearing foxholes can still be found and, here and there, the litter of war, ration cans, gas masks, ammunition etc. await discovery by future archeologists. Now and again, the forest gives up the remains of American or German dead, some of whose wartime friends still remember them. On a quiet sunny summer afternoon, down on the Jansbach creek, walkers can sometimes hear the distant sound of artillery or machine-gun fire emanating from the Belgian army camp and training area near Elsenborn. At Dom Bütgenbach, an obelisk lists the dead soldiers of the 1st Infantry Division who fell during the battle. Henry Warner's name

154. & 155. These two photos were found in a house in Krinkelt having been left there inside an ornate leather billfold by an unknown American soldier. Could it be that these people were his parents? (Author's collection)

can be seen although nothing tells the casual bystander that the young corporal single handedly knocked out three enemy tanks and caused a fourth to withdraw. Recognition of his valor came in the form of a posthumous Medal of Honor. Five other soldiers likewise earned the medal, Jose Lopez, Richard Cowan, Truman Kimbro, Vernon McGarity and William Soderman.

Last, but not least, the well-kept US military cemetery at Henri Chapelle is the final resting place of many who died in or near the Twin Villages during December of 1944.

Index

PLACES